NERUDA AND VALLEJO: SELECTED POEMS

NERUDA
AND
VALLEJO:
SELECTED
POEMS

Edited by
ROBERT BLY

Translations by
Robert Bly, John Knoepfle,
and James Wright

BEACON PRESS
Boston

Grateful acknowledgment is made to the following magazines in which some of these translations have appeared: *The London Magazine, The Nation, The Paris Review, Poetry, The Sixties, The University of Michigan Quarterly, Tri-Quarterly, Dragonfly, The Greenfield Review, Transpacific, Modern Occasions,* and *Crazy Horse.*

The translators would like to thank Hardie St. Martin for his generous criticism of these translations in manuscript

The drawings of Pablo Neruda and César Vallejo were done specially for the original Sixties Press editions by the Spanish artist Zamorano

Library of Congress catalog card number: 76–121825

International Standard Book Number: 0–8070–6420–3 (casebound)
0–8070–6421–1 (paperback)

Beacon Press books are published under the auspices of the Unitarian Universalist Association

Published simultaneously in Canada by Saunders of Toronto, Ltd.

Second printing, January 1972

CONTENTS

Selected Poems of Pablo Neruda

v

Selected Poems of César Vallejo

"Un pilar soportando consuelos"
"One pillar holding up consolations"

"Y no me digan nada"
"And don't bother telling me anything"

"¿Y bien? ¿Te sana el metaloide pálido?"
"And so? The pale metalloid heals you?"

"Tengo un miedo terrible de ser un animal"
"I have a terrible fear of being an animal"

"¡Y si después de tantas palabras"
"And what if after so many words"

"La cólera que quiebra al hombre en niños"
"The anger that breaks a man down into boys"

From ESPAÑA, APARTA DE MÍ ESTE CÁLIZ

Masa
Masses

Selected Poems of
PABLO NERUDA

ZAMORANO

REFUSING TO BE THEOCRITUS

Poets like St. John of the Cross and Juan Ramón Jiménez describe the single light shining at the center of all things. Neruda does not describe that light, and perhaps he does not see it. He describes instead the dense planets orbiting around it. As we open a Neruda book, we suddenly see going around us, in circles, like herds of mad buffalo or distracted horses, all sorts of created things; balconies, glacial rocks, lost address books, pipe organs, fingernails, notary publics, pumas, tongues of horses, shoes of dead people. His book, *Residencia En La Tierra* (*Living On Earth*—the Spanish title suggests being at home on the earth), contains an astounding variety of earthly things, that swim in a sort of murky water. The fifty-six poems in *Residencia I* and *II* were written over a period of ten years—roughly from the time Neruda was twenty-one until he was thirty-one, and they are the greatest surrealist poems yet written in a Western language. French surrealist poems appear drab and squeaky beside them. The French poets drove themselves by force into the unconscious because they hated establishment academicism and the rationalistic European culture. But Neruda has a gift, comparable to the fortune-teller's gift for living momentarily in the future, for living briefly in what we might call the unconscious present. Aragon and Breton are poets of reason, who occasionally throw themselves backward into the unconscious, but Neruda, like a deep-sea crab, all claws and shell, is able to breathe in the heavy substances that lie beneath the daylight consciousness. He stays on the bottom for hours, and moves around calmly and without hysteria.

The surrealist images in the *Residencia* poems arrange

3

themselves so as to embody curious and cunning ideas. In "La Calle Destruída," for example, he calls up injustice, architecture exploding, massive buildings weighing us down, exhausted religions, horses of pointless European armies—all of these things, he says, are acting so as to eat life for us, to destroy it, to disgust us so we will throw life away like old clothes. The poems give a sense of the ferocity and density of modern life.

Neruda's poetic master in the *Residencia* poems is not a European poet but the American, Walt Whitman. He looked deeply into Whitman. Whitman wrote:

> I see the workings of battle, pestilence, tyranny, I see
>   martyrs and prisoners,
> I observe a famine at sea, I observe the sailors casting
>   lots who shall be kill'd to preserve the lives of the
>   rest,
> I observe the slights and degradations cast by arrogant
>   persons upon laborers, the poor, and upon negroes,
>   and the like . . .
> I hear bravuras of birds, bustle of growing wheat,
>   gossip of flames, clack of sticks cooking my meals,
> I hear the sound I love, the sound of the human voice,
> I hear all sounds running together, combined, fused or
>   following . . .
> I hear the violoncello ('tis a young man's heart's com-
>   plaint),
> Hear the Key'd cornet, it glides quickly in through my
>   ears,
> It shakes mad-sweet pangs through my belly and
>   breast.

Neruda writes:

> I look at ships,
> I look at trees of bone marrow

4

bristling like mad cats,
I look at blood, daggers and women's stockings,
and men's hair,
I look at beds, I look at corridors where a virgin is
    sobbing,
I look at blankets and organs and hotels.

I look at secretive dreams,
I let the straggling days come in,
and the beginning also, and memories also,
like an eyelid held open hideously
I am watching.

And then this sound comes:
a red noise of bones,
a sticking together of flesh
and legs yellow as wheatheads meeting.
I am listening among the explosion of the kisses,
I am listening, shaken among breathings and sobs.

I am here, watching, listening,
with half of my soul at sea and half of my soul on land,
and with both halves of my soul I watch the world.

And even if I close my eyes and cover my heart over
    entirely,
I see the monotonous water falling
in big monotonous drops.
It is like a hurricane of gelatin,
like a waterfall of sperm and sea anemones.
I see a clouded rainbow hurrying.
I see its water moving over my bones.

He shows what it is like, not to be a poet, but to be alive.
The *Residencia* poems, however, differ from *Song of*

Myself in one fundamental way. The *Residencia* poems are weighed down by harshness, despair, loneliness, death, constant anxiety, loss. Whitman also wrote magnificently of the black emotions, but when Neruda in *Residencia* looks at the suicides, the drowning seamen, the blood-stained hair of the murdered girl, the scenes are not lightened by any sense of brotherhood. On the contrary, the animals and people on all sides isolate him still further, pull him down into his own body, where he struggles as though drowning in the stomach and the intestines.

It so happens I am sick of being a man . . .

I don't want to go on being a root in the dark,
insecure, stretched out, shivering with sleep,
going on down, into the moist guts of the earth,
taking in and thinking, eating every day . . .

I don't want so much misery.
I don't want to go on as a root and a tomb,
alone under the ground, a warehouse with corpses . . .

II

Pablo Neruda was born on July 12th, 1904, in a small frontier town in Southern Chile, the son of a railroad worker. The father was killed in a fall from his train while Neruda was still a boy. He said, "My father is buried in one of the rainiest cemeteries in the world." He described his childhood in Temuco in an essay called "Childhood and Poetry," printed as a preface to his Collected Poems. His given name was Neftali Beltran, and his pseudonym was taken very young out of admiration for a 19th century Czech writer.

In 1920, when he was sixteen, Neruda was sent off to Santiago for high school. His poem "Friends on The

Road" is written about those days. He was already com-
posing poems, a poetry of high animal spirits and en-
thusiasm. At nineteen, he published a book called *Twenty
Poems of Love and One Ode of Desperation*, which is still
loved all over South America.

> I remember you as you were that final autumn.
> You were a gray beret and the whole being at peace.
> In your eyes the fires of the evening dusk were battling,
> And the leaves were falling in the waters of your soul.

He said later that "love poems were sprouting out all
over my body."

> Body of a woman, white hills, white thighs,
> when you surrender, you stretch out like the world.
> My body, savage and peasant, undermines you
> and makes a son leap in the bottom of the earth.

In the preface to a short novel he wrote at this time, he
said: "In my day to day life, I am a tranquil man, the
enemy of laws, leaders, and established institutions. I find
the middle class odious, and I like the lives of people who
are restless and unsatisfied, whether they are artists or
criminals."

The governments of South America have a tradition of
encouraging young poets by offering them consular
posts. When Neruda was twenty-three, he was recognized
as a poet, and the Chilean government gave him a post
in the consular service in the Far East. During the next
five years, he lived in turn in Burma, Siam, China, Japan,
and India. Neruda remarks in the interview printed later
in this book that those years were years of great isolation
and loneliness. Many of the poems that appear in the first

two books of *Residencia En La Tierra* were written during those years.

Neruda came back to South America in 1932, when he was twenty-eight years old. For a while he was consul in Buenos Aires; he met Lorca there, when Lorca came to Argentina on a lecture tour. *Residencia I* was published in 1933. In 1934 he was assigned to Spain.

The Spanish poets had already known his wild poems for several years, and greeted him with admiration and enthusiasm. The house in Madrid where Neruda and his wife Delia lived soon became overflowing with poets—Lorca and Hernández especially loved to come. *Residencia II* was published in Spain in 1935. Lorca, Hernández and many others published their surrealist poems in Neruda's magazine *Caballo Verde por la Poesía* (Green Horse for Poetry). Spain had been for fifteen years in a great period of poetry, the most fertile for Spanish poetry since the 1500s. This period was brought to an end by the Civil War.

On July 19th, 1936, Franco invaded from North Africa. Neruda, overstepping his power as consul, immediately declared Chile on the side of the Spanish Republic. After being retired as Consul, he went to Paris, where he raised money for Spanish refugees, helped by Breton and other French poets, and by Vallejo. Neruda's poetry now became seriously political for the first time. Neruda had come to love Spain, living there, and he shared the shock of the Spanish poets, which was the shock of losing their country to the right wing. The growth of political energy in his poetry was probably inevitable in any case. In *Residencia I* and *II*, the outer world is seen with such clarity, and with such a sense of its suffering, that the later development of political poetry does not come as a surprise. He returned to America in 1940, and served as Chilean consul to Mexico

8

during 1941 and 1942. The poems he had written about
the Spanish Civil War were incorporated into *Residencia*,
under the title of *Residencia III*.

In 1944, the workers from Antofogasta, the nitrate
mining section of Chile, asked Neruda to run for Senator
from their district. He did, and was elected. He now
found himself in his country's Senate, as Yeats had. He
took a keen interest in Chilean politics. Several years
later he described in a long poem written to the Venezue-
lan poet, Miguel Otero Silva, how happy the Senators
would have been if he had remained a love poet:

When I was writing my love poems, which sprouted out
    from me
everywhere, and I was dying from depression,
nomadic, abandoned, gnawing the alphabet,
they said to me: "What a great man you are, Theocri-
    tus!"
I am not Theocritus: I took hold of life,
and faced her, and kissed her until I subdued her,
and then I went through the tunnels of the mines
to see how other men live.
And when I came out, my hands stained with depres-
    sion and garbage,
I held up my hands, and showed them to the generals,
and said, "I do not take responsibility for this crime."
They started to cough, became disgusted, left off say-
    ing hello,
gave up calling me Theocritus, and ended by insulting
    me
and assigning the entire police force to arrest me,
because I did not continue to be occupied exclusively
    with metaphysical subjects.

Neruda's experience as a Senator ended, as he mentions,
with his pursuit by the Secret Police. It came about in

this way: in 1948, González Videla, a right-wing strong man supported by United States interests, took over as dictator. Six months later Neruda, as Senator, attacked him for violations of the Chilean constitution. Videla responded by charging Neruda with treason. Neruda did not go into voluntary exile, as expected, but attacked Videla once more, and Videla ordered him arrested. Neruda went underground; miners and working people, to save his life, passed him from one house to another at night, first in Chile, later in other South American countries. He moved about for several months. Finally he crossed the Andes on horseback, and made it to Mexico; from there he flew out of the continent to Paris. All this time he was working on his new book, which he called *Canto General;* it was finished in February of 1949.

The title suggests a poetry that refuses to confine itself to a specific subject matter or kind of poem. Neruda worked on the book for fourteen years. It is the greatest long poem written on the American continent since *Leaves of Grass.* It is a geological, biological, and political history of South America. The book contains 340 poems arranged in fifteen sections. The fertility of imagination is astounding. Not all of the poems, of course, are of equal quality. In some, especially those written while Neruda was being hunted by the Chilean secret police, the anger breaks through the container of the poem. We are very slow about translating poetry in the United States, so it may be fifteen or twenty years before we have a translation of this book. For that reason, I have added in this small selection, along with the poems translated from *Canto General,* a very brief description of each section of Canto General, to give the reader some idea of the content and movement of the book.

The book as a whole gives a depressing picture of the relations between the U.S. State Department and South

American governments. Neruda's *Canto General* is not a great favorite of U.S. cultural organs dealing with Pan American relations. North Americans, both in universities and in the U.S.I.S., who know Neruda's work often say quite soberly that since Neruda became interested in politics, he has not written a poem of any value.

Neruda went from Paris to Russia for the one hundred fiftieth anniversary celebration of Pushkin's birth, and then back to Mexico, where the first edition of *Canto General* was published in 1950.

When González Videla's government fell, Neruda returned to Chile. Since 1953 he has lived on Isla Negra, a small island off the coast near Santiago; in recent years he has spent part of his time in Valparaiso also.

There was a considerable change in style from the inward, surrealist poems of *Residencia I* and *II* to the narrative, historical poems of *Canto General*. However, the style of his poetry has changed several more times since then. Both the *Residencia* and *Canto General* poems used, for the most part, the long loping line into which he could put so much power. In the middle 1950s he began writing odes using willowy lines only two or three words long. They were *Odas Elementales*, or "Odes to Simple Things." He wrote an ode to a wristwatch, which Jerome Rothenberg has translated very well, an ode to air, to his socks, to fire, to a watermelon, to printing, to salt. Book after book of these odes came out until he had published a hundred or so odes in three or four years. More recently he has embarked on a book of autobiographical poems called *Memorial to Isla Negra*.

At the moment, Neruda entirely dominates South American poetry. I heard a young South American poet complain of Neruda's abundance. He said that whenever a new idea appears in the air, and some younger poet manages to finish a poem on it, Neruda suddenly pub-

11

lishes three volumes! But, he said, "How can we be mad at Pablo? The poems continue to be good—that's the worst part of it!"

III

In "Childhood and Poetry," Neruda speculates on the origin of his poetry.

One time, investigating in the backyard of our house in Temuco the tiny objects and minuscule beings of my world, I came upon a hole in one of the boards of the fence. I looked through the hole and saw a landscape like that behind our house, uncared for, and wild. I moved back a few steps, because I sensed vaguely that something was about to happen. All of a sudden a hand appeared—a tiny hand of a boy about my own age. By the time I came close again, the hand was gone, and in its place there was a marvelous white sheep.

The sheep's wool was faded. Its wheels had escaped. All of this only made it more authentic. I had never seen such a wonderful sheep. I looked back through the hole but the boy had disappeared. I went into the house and brought out a treasure of my own: a pinecone, opened, full of odor and resin, which I adored. I set it down in the same spot and went off with the sheep.

I never saw either the hand or the boy again. And I have never again seen a sheep like that either. The toy I lost finally in a fire. But even now, in 1954, almost fifty years old, whenever I pass a toy shop, I look furtively into the window, but it's no use. They don't make sheep like that anymore.

I have been a lucky man. To feel the intimacy of brothers is a marvelous thing in life. To feel the love

12

of people whom we love is a fire that feeds our life. But to feel the affection that comes from those whom we do not know, from those unknown to us, who are watching over our sleep and solitude, over our dangers and our weaknesses—that is something still greater and more beautiful because it widens out the boundaries of our being, and unites all living things.

That exchange brought home to me for the first time a precious idea: that all of humanity is somehow together. That experience came to me again much later; this time it stood out strikingly against a background of trouble and persecution.

It won't surprise you then that I attempted to give something resiny, earthlike, and fragrant in exchange for human brotherhood. Just as I once left the pinecone by the fence, I have since left my words on the door of so many people who were unknown to me, people in prison, or hunted, or alone.

That is the great lesson I learned in my childhood, in the backyard of a lonely house. Maybe it was nothing but a game two boys played who didn't know each other and wanted to pass to the other some good things of life. Yet maybe this small and mysterious exchange of gifts remained inside me also, deep and indestructible, giving my poetry light.

This curious and beautiful story, which Neruda carefully links to the origins of his own poetry, is a conscious rejection of the connection between poetry and sickness, so often insisted on by Europeans. What is most startling about Neruda, I think, when we compare him to Eliot or Dylan Thomas or Pound, is the great affection that accompanies his imagination. Neruda read his poetry for the first time in the United States in June of 1966 at the

13

Poetry Center in New York, and it was clear from that reading that his poetry is intended as a gift. When Eliot gave a reading, one had the feeling that the reading was a cultural experience, and that Eliot doubted very much if you were worth the trouble, but he'd try anyway. When Dylan Thomas read, one had the sense that he was about to perform some magical and fantastic act, perhaps painting a Virgin while riding on three white horses, and maybe you would benefit from this act, and maybe you wouldn't. Pound used to scold the audience for not understanding what he did. When Neruda reads, the mood in the room is one of affection between the audience and himself.

IV

We tend to associate the modern imagination with the jerky imagination, which starts forward, stops, turns around, switches from subject to subject. In Neruda's poems, the imagination drives forward, joining the entire poem in a rising flow of imaginative energy. In the underworld of the consciousness, in the thickets where Freud, standing a short distance off, pointed out incest bushes, murder trees, half-buried primitive altars, and unburied bodies, Neruda's imagination moves with utter assurance, sweeping from one spot to another almost magically. The starved emotional lives of notary publics he links to the whiteness of flour, sexual desire to the shape of shoes, death to the barking sound where there is no dog. His imagination sees the hidden connections between conscious and unconscious substances with such assurance that he hardly bothers with metaphors—he links them by tying their hidden tails. He is a new kind of creature moving about under the surface of everything. Moving under the earth, he knows everything from the bottom up (which is the right way to learn the nature

14

of a thing) and therefore is never at a loss for its name. Compared to him, most American poets resemble blind men moving gingerly along the ground from tree to tree, from house to house, feeling each thing for a long time, and then calling out "House!" when we already know it is a house.

Neruda has confidence in what is hidden. The Establishment respects only what the light has fallen on, but Neruda likes the unlit just as well. He writes of small typists without scorn, and of the souls of huge, sleeping snakes.

He violates the rules for behavior set up by the wise. The conventionally wise assure us that to a surrealist the outer world has no reality—only his inner flow of images is real. Neruda's work demolishes this banality. Neruda's poetry is deeply surrealist, and yet entities of the outer world like the United Fruit Company have greater force in his poems than in those of any strictly "outward" poet alive. Once a poet takes a political stand, the wise assure us that he will cease writing good poetry. Neruda became a Communist in the middle of his life and has remained one: at least half of his greatest work, one must admit, was written after that time. He has written great poetry at all times of his life.

Finally, many critics in the United States insist the poem must be hard-bitten, impersonal, and rational, lest it lack sophistication. Neruda is wildly romantic, and more sophisticated than Hulme or Pound could dream of being. He has few literary theories. Like Vallejo, Neruda wishes to help humanity, and tells the truth for that reason.

Robert Bly

15

from

Veinte Poemas
de Amor y Una Canción
Desesperada

*(Twenty Poems of Love and
One Ode of Desperation)*

1924

Cuerpo de mujer, blancas colinas, muslos blancos
te pareces al mundo en tu actitud de entrega.
Mi cuerpo de labriego salvaje te socava
y hace saltar el hijo del fondo de la tierra.

Fuí solo como un túnel. De mí huían los pájaros,
y en mí la noche entraba su invasión poderosa.
Para sobrevivirme te forjé como un arma,
como una flecha en mi arco, como una piedra en mi honda.

Pero cae la hora de la venganza, y te amo.
Cuerpo de piel, de musgo, de leche ávida y firme.
Ah los vasos del pecho! Ah los ojos de ausencia!
Ah las rosas del pubis! Ah tu voz lenta y triste!

Cuerpo de mujer mía, persistiré en tu gracia.
Mi sed, mi ansia sin límite, mi camino indeciso!
Oscuros cauces donde la sed eterna sigue,
y la fatiga sigue, y el dolor infinito.

Body of a woman, white hills, white thighs,
when you surrender, you stretch out like the world.
My body, savage and peasant, undermines you
and makes a son leap in the bottom of the earth.

I was lonely as a tunnel. Birds flew from me.
And night invaded me with her powerful army.
To survive I forged you like a weapon,
like an arrow for my bow, or a stone for my sling.

But now the hour of revenge falls, and I love you.
Body of skin, of moss, of firm and thirsty milk!
And the cups of your breasts! And your eyes full of
    absence!
And the roses of your mound! And your voice slow and
    sad!

Body of my woman, I will live on through your marvel-
    ousness.
My thirst, my desire without end, my wavering road!
Dark river beds down which the eternal thirst is flowing,
and the fatigue is flowing, and the grief without shore.

Translated by Robert Bly

Te recuerdo como eras en el último otoño.
Eras la boina gris y el corazón en calma.
En tus ojos peleaban las llamas del crepúsculo.
Y las hojas caían en el agua de tu alma.

Apegada a mis brazos como una enredadera,
las hojas recogían tu voz lenta y en calma.
Hoguera de estupor en que mi sed ardía.
Dulce jacinto azul torcido sobre mi alma.

Siento viajar tus ojos y es distante el otoño:
boina gris, voz de pájaro y corazón de casa
hacia donde emigraban mis profundos anhelos
y caían mis besos alegres como brasas.

Cielo desde un navío. Campo desde los cerros:
Tu recuerdo es de luz, de humo, de estanque en calma!
Más allá de tus ojos ardían los crepúsculos.
Hojas secas de otoño giraban en tu alma.

I remember you as you were that final autumn.
You were a gray beret and the whole being at peace.
In your eyes the fires of the evening dusk were battling,
and the leaves were falling in the waters of your soul.

As attached to my arms as a morning glory,
your sad, slow voice was picked up by the leaves.
Bonfire of astonishment in which my thirst was burning.
Soft blue of hyacinth twisting above my soul.

I feel your eyes travel and the autumn is distant:
gray beret, voice of a bird, and heart like a house
toward which my profound desires were emigrating
and my thick kisses were falling like hot coals.

The sky from a ship. The plains from a hill:
your memory is of light, of smoke, of a still pool!
Beyond your eyes the evening dusks were battling.
Dry leaves of autumn were whirling in your soul.

Translated by Robert Bly

from

Residencia en
la Tierra
I and II

1925–1935

SOLO LA MUERTE

Hay cementerios solos,
tumbas llenas de huesos sin sonido,
el corazón pasando un túnel
oscuro, oscuro, oscuro,
como un naufragio hacia adentro nos morimos,
como ahogarnos en el corazón,
como irnos cayendo desde la piel al alma.

Hay cadáveres,
hay pies de pegajosa losa fría,
hay la muerte en los huesos,
como un sonido puro,
como un ladrido sin perro,
saliendo de ciertas campanas, de ciertas tumbas
creciendo en la humedad como el llanto a la lluvia.

Yo veo, solo, a veces,
ataúdes a vela
zarpar con difuntos pálidos, con mujeres de trenzas
    muertas,
con panaderos blancos como ángeles,
con niñas pensativas casadas con notarios,
ataúdes subiendo el río vertical de los muertos,
el río morado,
hacia arriba, con las velas hinchadas por el sonido de la
    muerte,
hinchadas por el sonido silencioso de la muerte.

A lo sonoro llega la muerte
como un zapato sin pie, como un traje sin hombre,
llega a golpear con un anillo sin piedra y sin dedo,

NOTHING BUT DEATH

There are cemeteries that are lonely,
graves full of bones that do not make a sound,
the heart moving through a tunnel,
in it darkness, darkness, darkness,
like a shipwreck we die going into ourselves,
as though we were drowning inside our hearts,
as though we lived falling out of the skin into the soul.

And there are corpses,
feet made of cold and sticky clay,
death is inside the bones,
like a barking where there are no dogs,
coming out from bells somewhere, from graves somewhere,
growing in the damp air like tears or rain.

Sometimes I see alone
coffins under sail,
embarking with the pale dead, with women that have dead
    hair,
with bakers who are as white as angels,
and pensive young girls married to notary publics,
caskets sailing up the vertical river of the dead,
the river of dark purple,
moving upstream with sails filled out by the sound of
    death,
filled by the sound of death which is silence.

Death arrives among all that sound
like a shoe with no foot in it, like a suit with no man in it,
comes and knocks, using a ring with no stone in it, with no
    finger in it,

llega a gritar sin boca, sin lengua, sin garganta.
Sin embargo sus pasos suenan
y su vestido suena, callado, como un árbol.

Yo no sé, yo conozco poco, yo apenas veo,
pero creo que su canto tiene color de violetas húmedas,
de violetas acostumbradas a la tierra,
porque la cara de la muerte es verde,
y la mirada de la muerte es verde,
con la aguda humedad de una hoja de violeta
y su grave color de invierno exasperado.

Pero la muerte va también por el mundo vestida de escoba,
lame el suelo buscando difuntos,
la muerte está en la escoba,
es la lengua de la muerte buscando muertos,
es la aguja de la muerte buscando hilo.

La muerte está en los catres:
en los colchones lentos, en las frazadas negras
vive tendida, y de repente sopla:
sopla un sonido oscuro que hincha sábanas,
y hay camas navegando a un puerto
en donde está esperando, vestida de almirante.

comes and shouts with no mouth, with no tongue, with no
     throat.
Nevertheless its steps can be heard
and its clothing makes a hushed sound, like a tree.

I'm not sure, I understand only a little, I can hardly see,
but it seems to me that its singing has the color of damp
     violets,
of violets that are at home in the earth,
because the face of death is green,
and the look death gives is green,
with the penetrating dampness of a violet leaf
and the somber color of embittered winter.

But death also goes through the world dressed as a broom,
lapping the floor, looking for dead bodies,
death is inside the broom,
the broom is the tongue of death looking for corpses,
it is the needle of death looking for thread.

Death is inside the folding cots:
it spends its life sleeping on the slow mattresses,
in the black blankets, and suddenly breathes out:
it blows out a mournful sound that swells the sheets,
and the beds go sailing toward a port
where death is waiting, dressed like an admiral.

Translated by Robert Bly

WALKING AROUND

Sucede que me canso de ser hombre.
Sucede que entro en las sastrerías y en los cines
marchito, impenetrable, como un cisne de fieltro
navegando en un agua de origen y ceniza.

El olor de las peluquerías me hace llorar a gritos.
Sólo quiero un descanso de piedras o de lana,
sólo quiero no ver establecimientos ni jardines,
ni mercaderías, ni anteojos, ni ascensores.

Sucede que me canso de mis pies y mis uñas
y mi pelo y mi sombra.
Sucede que me canso de ser hombre.

Sin embargo sería delicioso
asustar a un notario con un lirio cortado
o dar muerte a una monja con un golpe de oreja.
Sería bello
ir por las calles con un cuchillo verde
y dando gritos hasta morir de frío.

No quiero seguir siendo raíz en las tinieblas,
vacilante, extendido, tiritando de sueño,
hacia abajo, en las tapias mojadas de la tierra,
absorbiendo y pensando, comiendo cada día.

No quiero para mí tantas desgracias.
No quiero continuar de raíz y de tumba,
de subterráneo solo, de bodega con muertos,
aterido, muriéndome de pena.

WALKING AROUND

It so happens I am sick of being a man.
And it happens that I walk into tailorshops and movie
    houses
dried up, waterproof, like a swan made of felt
steering my way in a water of wombs and ashes.

The smell of barbershops makes me break into hoarse
    sobs.
The only thing I want is to lie still like stones or wool.
The only thing I want is to see no more stores, no gardens,
no more goods, no spectacles, no elevators.

It so happens I am sick of my feet and my nails
and my hair and my shadow.
It so happens I am sick of being a man.

Still it would be marvelous
to terrify a law clerk with a cut lily,
or kill a nun with a blow on the ear.
It would be great
to go through the streets with a green knife
letting out yells until I died of the cold.

I don't want to go on being a root in the dark,
insecure, stretched out, shivering with sleep,
going on down, into the moist guts of the earth,
taking in and thinking, eating every day.

I don't want so much misery.
I don't want to go on as a root and a tomb,
alone under the ground, a warehouse with corpses,
half frozen, dying of grief.

Por eso el día lunes arde como el petróleo
cuando me ve llegar con mi cara de cárcel,
y aúlla en su transcurso como una rueda herida,
y da pasos de sangre caliente hacia la noche.

Y me empuja a ciertos rincones, a ciertas casas húmedas,
a hospitales donde los huesos salen por la ventana,
a ciertas zapaterías con olor a vinagre,
a calles espantosas como grietas.

Hay pájaros de color de azufre y horribles intestinos
colgando de las puertas de las casas que odio,
hay dentaduras olvidadas en una cafetera,
hay espejos
que debieran haber llorado de vergüenza y espanto,
hay paraguas en todas partes, y venenos, y ombligos.

Yo paseo con calma, con ojos, con zapatos,
con furia, con olvido,
paso, cruzo oficinas y tiendas de ortopedia,
y patios donde hay ropas colgadas de un alambre:
calzoncillos, toallas y camisas que lloran
lentas lágrimas sucias.

That's why Monday, when it sees me coming
with my convict face, blazes up like gasoline,
and it howls on its way like a wounded wheel,
and leaves tracks full of warm blood leading toward the
    night.

And it pushes me into certain corners, into some moist
    houses,
into hospitals where the bones fly out the window,
into shoeshops that smell like vinegar,
and certain streets hideous as cracks in the skin.

There are sulphur-colored birds, and hideous intestines
hanging over the doors of houses that I hate,
and there are false teeth forgotten in a coffeepot,
there are mirrors
that ought to have wept from shame and terror,
there are umbrellas everywhere, and venoms, and umbili-
    cal cords.

I stroll along serenely, with my eyes, my shoes,
my rage, forgetting everything,
I walk by, going through office buildings and orthopedic
    shops,
and courtyards with washing hanging from the line:
underwear, towels and shirts from which slow
dirty tears are falling.

                                Translated by Robert Bly

ARTE POÉTICA

Entre sombra y espacio, entre guarniciones y doncellas,
dotado de corazón singular y sueños funestos,
precipitadamente pálido, marchito en la frente
y con luto de viudo furioso por cada día de mi vida,
ay, para cada agua invisible que bebo soñolientamente
y de todo sonido que acojo temblando,
tengo la misma sed ausente y la misma fiebre fría
un oído que nace, una angustia indirecta,
como si llegaran ladrones o fantasmas,
y en una cáscara de extensión fija y profunda,
como un camarero humillado, como una campana un poco
    ronca,
como un espejo viejo, como un olor de casa sola
en la que los huéspedes entran de noche perdidamente
    ebrios,
y hay un olor de ropa tirada al suelo, y una ausencia de
    flores
—posiblemente de otro modo aún menos melancólico—,
pero, la verdad, de pronto, el viento que azota mi pecho,
las noches de substancia infinita caídas en mi dormitorio,
el ruido de un día que arde con sacrificio
me piden lo profético que hay en mí, con melancolía
y un golpe de objetos que llaman sin ser respondidos
hay, y un movimiento sin tregua, y un nombre confuso.

THE ART OF POETRY

Between shadows and clearing, between defenses and
    young girls,
having inherited an original heart, and funereal imagina-
    tion,
suddenly pale, something withered in my face,
in mourning like a desperate widower every day of my
    life,
for every drop of invisible water I drink
in my sleepy way, and for every sound I take in shivering,
I have the same chilly fever, and the same absent thirst,
an ear coming into the world, an oblique anxiety,
as though robbers were about to arrive, or ghosts,
inside a seashell with great and unchangeable depths,
like a humiliated waiter, or a bell slightly hoarse,
like an aged mirror or the smell of an empty house
where the guests come in hopelessly drunk at night,
having an odor of clothes thrown on the floor, and no
    flowers,
—in another sense, possibly not as sad—
still, the truth is, the wind suddenly hitting my chest,
the nights with infinite substance fallen into my bedroom,
the crackling of a day hardly able to burn,
ask from me sadly whatever I have that is prophetic,
and there are objects that knock, and are never answered,
and something always moving, and a name that does not
    come clear.

Translated by Robert Bly

ENTIERRO EN EL ESTE

Yo trabajo de noche, rodeado de ciudad,
de pescadores, de alfareros, de difuntos quemados
con azafrán y frutas, envueltos en muselina escarlata:
bajo mi balcón esos muertos terribles
pasan sonando cadenas y flautas de cobre,
estridentes y finas y lúgubres silban
entre el color de las pesadas flores envenenadas
y el grito de los cenicientos danzarines
y el creciente monótono de los tamtam
y el humo de las maderas que arden y huelen.

Porque una vez doblado el camino, junto al turbio río,
sus corazones, detenidos o iniciando un mayor movimiento
rodarán quemados, con la pierna y el pie hechos fuego,
y la trémula ceniza caerá sobre el agua,
flotará como ramo de flores calcinadas
o como extinto fuego dejado por tan poderosos viajeros
que hicieron arder algo sobre las negras aguas, y
    devoraron
un aliento desaparecido y un licor extremo.

FUNERAL IN THE EAST

I work at night, the city all around me,
fishermen, and potters, and corpses that are burned
with saffron and fruit, rolled in scarlet muslin:
those terrifying corpses go past under my balcony,
making their chains and copper flutes give off noise,
whistling sounds, harsh and pure and mournful,
among the brightness of the flowers heavy and poisoned,
and the cries of the dancers covered with ashes,
and the constantly rising monotony of the drum,
and the smoke from the logs scented and burning.

For once around the corner, near the muddy river,
their hearts, either stopping or starting off at a greater
        speed,
will roll over, burned, the leg and the foot turned to fire,
and the fluttering ashes will settle down on the water
and float like a branch of chalky flowers,
or like an extinct fire left by travelers with such great
        powers
they made something blaze up on the black waters, and
        bolted down
a food no longer found, and one finishing drink.

Translated by Robert Bly

CABALLERO SOLO

Los jóvenes homosexuales y las muchachas amorosas,
y las largas viudas que sufren el delirante insomnio,
y las jóvenes señoras preñadas hace treinta horas,
y los roncos gatos que cruzan mi jardín en tinieblas,
como un collar de palpitantes ostras sexuales
rodean mi residencia solitaria,
como enemigos establecidos contra mi alma,
como conspiradores en traje de dormitorio
que cambiaran largos besos espesos por consigna.

El radiante verano conduce a los enamorados
en uniformes regimientos melancólicos,
hechos de gordas y flacas y alegres y tristes parejas:
bajo los elegantes cocoteros, junto al océano y la luna,
hay una continua vida de pantalones y polleras,
un rumor de medias de seda acariciadas,
y senos femeninos que brillan como ojos.

El pequeño empleado, después de mucho,
después del tedio semanal, y las novelas leídas de noche en
    cama,
ha definitivamente seducido a su vecina,
y la lleva a los miserables cinematógrafos
donde los héroes son potros o príncipes apasionados,
y acaricia sus piernas llenas de dulce vello
con sus ardientes y húmedas manos que huelen a ciga-
    rrillo.

GENTLEMAN WITHOUT COMPANY

The homosexual young men and the love-mad girls,
and the long widows who suffer from a delirious inability
    to sleep,
and the young wives who have been pregnant for thirty
    hours,
and the hoarse cats that cross my garden in the dark,
these, like a necklace of throbbing sexual oysters,
surround my solitary house,
like enemies set up against my soul,
like members of a conspiracy dressed in sleeping cos-
    tumes,
who give each other as passwords long and profound
    kisses.

The shining summer leads out the lovers
in low-spirited regiments that are all alike,
made up of fat and thin and cheerful and sullen pairs;
under the elegant coconut palms, near the sea and the
    moon,
there is a steady movement of trousers and petticoats,
and a hum from the stroking of silk stockings,
and women's breasts sparkling like eyes.

The small-time employee, after many things,
after the boredom of the week, and the novels read in bed
    at night,
has once and for all seduced the woman next door,
and now he escorts her to the miserable movies,
where the heroes are either colts or passionate princes,
and he strokes her legs sheathed in their sweet down
with his warm and damp hands that smell of cigarettes.

Los atardeceres del seductor y las noches de los esposos
se unen como dos sábanas sepultándome
y las horas después del almuerzo en que los jóvenes
    estudiantes
y las jóvenes estudiantes, y los sacerdotes se masturban,
y los animales fornican directamente,
y las abejas huelen a sangre, y las moscas zumban
    coléricas,
y los primos juegan extrañamente con sus primas,
y los médicos miran con furia al marido de la joven
    paciente,
y las horas de la mañana en que el profesor, como por
    descuido,
cumple con su deber conyugal y desayuna,
y más aún, los adúlteros, que se aman con verdadero amor
sobre lechos altos y largos como embarcaciones:
seguramente, eternamente me rodea
este gran bosque respiratorio y enredado
con grandes flores como bocas y dentaduras
y negras raíces en forma de uñas y zapatos.

The evenings of the woman-chaser and the nights of the
    husbands
come together like two bed-sheets and bury me,
and the hours after lunch, when the young male students
and the young women students, and the priests are
    masturbating,
and the animals are riding each other frankly,
and the bees have an odor of blood, and the flies buzz in
    anger,
and cousins play strange games with their girl-cousins,
and doctors look with rage at the husband of the young
    patient,
and the morning hours, when the professor, as if absent-
    minded,
performs his marital duty, and has breakfast,
and still more, the adulterers, who love each other with
    a real love
on beds high and huge as ocean liners,
this immense forest, entangled and breathing,
hedges me around firmly on all sides forever
with huge flowers like mouths and rows of teeth
and black roots that look like fingernails and shoes.

Translated by Robert Bly

SONATA Y DESTRUCCIONES

Después de mucho, después de vagas leguas,
confuso de dominios, incierto de territorios,
acompañado de pobres esperanzas
y compañías infieles y desconfiados sueños,
amo lo tenaz que aún sobrevive en mis ojos,
oigo en mi corazón mis pasos de jinete,
muerdo el fuego dormido y la sal arruinada,
y de noche, de atmósfera oscura y luto prófugo,
aquel que vela a la orilla de los campamentos,
el viajero armado de estériles resistencias,
detenido entre sombras que crecen y alas que tiemblan,
me siento ser, y mi brazo de piedra me defiende.

Hay entre ciencias de llanto un altar confuso,
y en mi sesión de atardeceres sin perfume,
en mis abandonados dormitorios donde habita la luna,
y arañas de mi propiedad, y destrucciones que me son
        queridas,
adoro mi propio ser perdido, mi substancia imperfecta,
mi golpe de plata y mi pérdida eterna.
Ardió la uva húmeda, y su agua funeral
aún vacila, aún reside,
y el patrimonio estéril, y el domicilio traidor.
Quién hizo ceremonia de cenizas?

Quién amó lo perdido, quién protegió lo último?
El hueso del padre, la madera del buque muerto,
y su propio final, su misma huída,
su fuerza triste, su dios miserable?

SONATA AND DESTRUCTIONS

After so many things, after so many hazy miles,
not sure which kingdom it is, not knowing the terrain,
traveling with pitiful hopes,
and lying companions, and suspicious dreams,
I love the firmness that still survives in my eyes,
I hear my heart beating as if I were riding a horse,
I bite the sleeping fire and the ruined salt,
and at night, when darkness is thick, and mourning
    furtive,
I imagine I am the one keeping watch on the far shore
of the encampments, the traveler armed with his sterile
    defenses,
caught between growing shadows
and shivering wings, and my arm made of stone protects
    me.

There's a confused altar among the sciences of tears,
and in my twilight meditations with no perfume,
and in my deserted sleeping rooms where the moon lives,
and the spiders that belong to me, and the destructions I
    am fond of,
I love my own lost self, my faulty stuff,
my silver wound, and my eternal loss.
The damp grapes burned, and their funereal water
is still flickering, is still with us,
and the sterile inheritance, and the treacherous home.
Who performed a ceremony of ashes?

Who loved the lost thing, who sheltered the last thing of
    all?
The father's bone, the dead ship's timber,
and his own end, his flight,
his melancholy power, his god that had bad luck?

41

Acecho, pues, lo inanimado y lo doliente,
y el testimonio extraño que sostengo,
con eficiencia cruel y escrito en cenizas,
es la forma de olvido que prefiero,
el nombre que doy a la tierra, el valor de mis sueños,
la cantidad interminable que divido
con mis ojos de invierno, durante cada día de este mundo.

I lie in wait, then, for what is not alive and what is
     suffering,
and the extraordinary testimony I bring forward,
with brutal efficiency and written down in the ashes,
is the form of oblivion that I prefer,
the name I give to the earth, the value of my dreams,
the endless abundance which I distribute
with my wintry eyes, every day this world goes on.

Translated by Robert Bly

LA CALLE DESTRUÍDA

Por el hierro injuriado, por los ojos del yeso
pasa una lengua de años diferentes
del tiempo. Es una cola
de ásperas crines, unas manos de piedra llenas de ira,
y el color de las casas enmudece, y estallan
las decisiones de la arquitectura,
un pie terrible ensucia los balcones:
con lentitud, con sombra acumulada,
con máscaras mordidas de invierno y lentitud,
se pasean los días de alta frente
entre casas sin luna.

El agua y la costumbre y el lodo blanco
que la estrella despide, y en especial
el aire que las campas han golpeado con furia
gastan las cosas, tocan
las ruedas, se detienen
en las cigarrerías,
y crece el pelo rojo con las cornisas
como un largo lamento, mientras a lo profundo
caen llaves, relojes,
flores asimiladas al olvido.

Dónde está la violeta recién parida? Dónde
la corbata y el virginal céfiro rojo?
Sobre las poblaciones
una lengua de polvo podrido se adelanta
rompiendo anillos, royendo pintura,
haciendo aullar sin voz las sillas negras,
cubriendo los florones del cemento, los baluartes
de metal destrozado,

THE RUINED STREET

A tongue from different eras of time is moving
over the injured iron, over the eyes
of plaster. It's a tail of harsh
horsehair, stone hands stuffed with rage,
and the house colors fall silent, and the decisions
of the architecture explode,
a ghastly foot makes the balconies filthy,
so slowly, with saved-up shadow,
with face masks bitten by winter and leisure,
the days with their high foreheads drift between
the houses with no moon.

The water and the customs and the white mud
that the star sprinkles down, and especially
the air that the bells have beaten in their rage
are wearing things out, brushing
the wheels, pausing
at the cigarshops,
and red hair grows on the cornices
like a long sorrow, while keys are falling
into the hole, watches,
and flowers adjusted to nothingness.

Where is the newly born violet? Where are
the necktie and the virginal red yarn?
A tongue of rotten dust is moving forward
over the cities
smashing rings, eating away the paint,
making the black chairs howl soundlessly,
burying the cement florals, the parapets
of mangled metal,

el jardín y la lana, las ampliaciones de fotografías
    ardientes
heridas por la lluvia, la sed de las alcobas, y los grandes
carteles de los cines en donde luchan
la pantera y el trueno,
las lanzas del geranio, los almacenes llenos de miel
    perdida,
la tos, los trajes de tejido brillante,
todo se cubre de un sabor mortal
a retroceso y humedad y herida.

Tal vez las conversaciones anudadas, el roce de los
    cuerpos,
la virtud de las fatigadas señoras que anidan en el humo,
los tomates asesinados implacablemente,
el paso de los caballos de un triste regimiento,
la luz, la presión de muchos dedos sin nombre
gastan la fibra plana de la cal,
rodean de aire neutro las fachadas
como cuchillos: mientras
el aire del peligro roe las circunstancias,
los ladrillos, la sal se derrama como aguas
y los carros de gordos ejes tambalean.

Ola de rosas rotas y agujeros! Futuro
de la vena olorosa! Objetos sin piedad!
Nadie circule! Nadie abra los brazos
dentro del agua ciega!
Oh movimiento, oh nombre malherido,
oh cucharada de viento confuso
y color azotado! Oh herida en donde caen
hasta morir las guitarras azules!

the orchard and the wool, the fiery and blown-up photo-
      graphs
injured by the rain, the thirst of the bedrooms, and the
      huge
movie posters in which the panther
is wrestling with thunder,
the geranium-spears, granaries full of lost honey,
the cough, the suits with their metallic threads,
everything gets covered with a deathly flavor
of regression and dampness and damage.

It's possible that the conversations now underway, the
      bodies brushing,
the chastity of the tired ladies who make their nest in the
      smoke,
the tomatoes murdered without mercy,
the horses of a depressed regiment going by,
the light, the pressure of nameless fingertips
are wearing out the flat fiber of the lime,
surrounding the building fronts with neuter air
like knives: while
the dangerous air goes chewing up the way we stay alive,
the bricks, the salt runs over like waters,
and the carts with fat axles go bumping by.

Surf of broken roses and tiny holes! Future
of the perfumed vein! Merciless objects!
Do not move, anyone! Do not open your arms
while in the blind water!
Oh motion, oh name that is gravely wounded,
oh spoonful of bewildered wind,
and knocked-around color! Oh wound into which
the blue guitars fall and are killed!

Translated by Robert Bly

MELANCOLÍA EN LAS FAMILIAS

Conservo un frasco azul,
dentro de él una oreja y un retrato:
cuando la noche obliga
a las plumas del buho,
cuando el ronco cerezo
se destroza los labios y amenaza
con cáscaras que el viento del océano a menudo perfora,
yo sé que hay grandes extensiones hundidas,
cuarzo en lingotes,
cieno,
aguas azules para una batalla,
mucho silencio, muchas
vetas de retrocesos y alcanfores,
cosas caídas, medallas, ternuras,
paracaídas, besos.

No es sino el paso de un día hacia otro,
una sola botella andando por los mares,
y un comedor adonde llegan rosas,
un comedor abandonado
como una espina: me refiero
a una copa trizada, a una cortina, al fondo
de una sala desierta por donde pasa un río
arrastrando las piedras. Es una casa
situada en los cimientos de la lluvia,
una casa de dos pisos con ventanas obligatorias
y enredaderas estrictamente fieles.

Voy por las tardes, llego
lleno de lodo y muerte,

MELANCHOLY INSIDE FAMILIES

I keep a blue bottle.
Inside it an ear and a portrait.
When the night dominates
the feathers of the owl,
when the hoarse cherry tree
rips out its lips and makes menacing gestures
with rinds which the ocean wind often perforates—
then I know that there are immense expanses hidden from
    us,
quartz in slugs,
ooze,
blue waters for a battle,
much silence, many ore-veins
of withdrawals and camphor,
fallen things, medallions, kindnesses,
parachutes, kisses.

It is only the passage from one day to another,
a single bottle moving over the seas,
and a dining room where roses arrive,
a dining room deserted
as a fish-bone; I am speaking of
a smashed cup, a curtain, at the end
of a deserted room through which a river passes
dragging along the stones. It is a house
set on the foundations of the rain,
a house of two floors with the required number of windows,
and climbing vines faithful in every particular.

I walk through afternoons, I arrive
full of mud and death,

arrastrando la tierra y sus raíces,
y su vaga barriga en donde duermen
cadáveres con trigo,
metales, elefantes derrumbados.

Pero por sobre todo hay un terrible,
un terrible comedor abandonado,
con las alcuzas rotas
y el vinagre corriendo debajo de las sillas,
un rayo detenido de la luna,
algo oscuro, y me busco
una comparación dentro de mí:
tal vez es una tienda rodeada por el mar
y paños rotos goteando salmuera.

Es sólo un comedor abandonado,
y alrededor hay extensiones,
fábricas sumergidas, maderas
que sólo yo conozco,
porque estoy triste y viajo,
y conozco la tierra, y estoy triste.

dragging along the earth and its roots,
and its indistinct stomach in which corpses
are sleeping with wheat,
metals, and pushed-over elephants.

But above all there is a terrifying,
a terrifying deserted dining room,
with its broken olive oil cruets,
and vinegar running under its chairs,
one ray of moonlight tied down,
something dark, and I look
for a comparison inside myself:
perhaps it is a grocery store surrounded by the sea
and torn clothing from which sea water is dripping.

It is only a deserted dining room,
and around it there are expanses,
sunken factories, pieces of timber
which I alone know,
because I am sad, and because I travel,
and I know the earth, and I am sad.

Translated by Robert Bly
and James Wright

AGUA SEXUAL

Rodando a goterones solos,
a gotas como dientes,
a espesos goterones de mermelada y sangre,
rodando a goterones,
cae el agua,
como una espada en gotas,
como un desgarrador río de vidrio,
cae mordiendo,
golpeando el eje de la simetría, pegando en las costuras
    del alma,
rompiendo cosas abandonadas, empapando lo oscuro.

Solamente es un soplo, más húmedo que que el llanto,
un líquido, un sudor, un aceite sin nombre,
un movimiento agudo,
haciéndose, espesándose,
cae el agua,
a goterones lentos,
hacia su mar, hacia su seco océano,
hacia su ola sin agua.

Veo el verano extenso, y un estertor saliendo de un
    granero,
bodegas, cigarras,
poblaciones, estímulos,
habitaciones, niñas
durmiendo con las manos en el corazón,
soñando con bandidos, con incendios,
veo barcos,
veo árboles de médula
erizados como gatos rabiosos,

52

SEXUAL WATER

Rolling down in big and distinct drops,
in drops like teeth,
in heavy drops like marmalade and blood,
rolling down in big drops, the water
is falling,
like a sword made of drops,
like a river of glass that tears things,
it is falling, biting,
beating on the axle of symmetry, knocking on the seams
    of the soul,
breaking abandoned things, soaking the darkness.

It is nothing but a breath, more full of moisture than
    crying,
a liquid, a sweat, an oil that has no name,
a sharp motion,
taking shape, making itself thick,
the water is falling
in slow drops
toward the sea, toward its dry ocean,
toward its wave without water.

I look at the wide summer, and a loud noise coming from
    a barn,
wineshops, cicadas,
towns, excitements,
houses, girls
sleeping with hands over their hearts,
dreaming of pirates, of conflagrations,
I look at ships,
I look at trees of bone marrow
bristling like mad cats,

veo sangre, puñales y medias de mujer,
y pelos de hombre,
veo camas, veo corredores donde grita una virgen,
veo frazadas y órganos y hoteles.

Veo los sueños sigilosos,
admito los postreros días,
y también los origenes, y también los recuerdos,
como un párpado atrozmente levantado a la fuerza
estoy mirando.

Y entonces hay este sonido:
un ruido rojo de huesos,
un pegarse de carne,
y piernas amarillas como espigas juntándose.
Yo escucho entre el disparo de los besos,
escucho, sacudido entre respiraciones y sollozos.

Estoy, mirando, oyendo,
con la mitad del alma en el mar y la mitad del alma en la
        tierra,
y con las dos mitades del alma miro el mundo.

Y aunque cierre los ojos y me cubra el corazon entera-
        mente,
veo caer un agua sorda,
a goterones sordos.
Es como un huracán de gelatina,
como una catarata de espermas y medusas.
Veo correr un arco iris turbio.
Veo pasar sus aguas a través de los huesos.

I look at blood, daggers and women's stockings,
and men's hair,
I look at beds, I look at corridors where a virgin is
    sobbing,
I look at blankets and organs and hotels.

I look at secretive dreams,
I let the straggling days come in,
and the beginnings also, and memories also,
like an eyelid held open hideously
I am watching.

And then this sound comes:
a red noise of bones,
a sticking together of flesh
and legs yellow as wheatheads meeting.
I am listening among the explosion of the kisses,
I am listening, shaken among breathings and sobs.

I am here, watching, listening,
with half of my soul at sea and half of my soul on land,
and with both halves of my soul I watch the world.

And even if I close my eyes and cover my heart over
    entirely,
I see the monotonous water falling
in big monotonous drops.
It is like a hurricane of gelatin,
like a waterfall of sperm and sea anemones.
I see a clouded rainbow hurrying.
I see its water moving over my bones.

Translated by James Wright
and Robert Bly

NO HAY OLVIDO
(*Sonata*)

Si me preguntáis en donde he estado
debo decir "Sucede".
Debo de hablar del suelo que oscurecen las piedras,
del río que durando se destruye:
no sé sino las cosas que los pájaros pierden,
el mar dejado atrás, o mi hermana llorando.
Por qué tantas regiones, por qué un día
se junta con un día? Por qué una negra noche
se acumula en la boca? Por qué muertos?

Si me preguntáis de donde vengo, tengo que conversar
        con cosas rotas,
con utensilios demasiado amargos,
con grandes bestias a menudo podridas
y con mi acongojado corazón.

No son recuerdos los que se han cruzado
ni es la paloma amarillenta que duerme en el olvido,
sino caras con lágrimas,
dedos en la garganta,
y lo que se desploma de las hojas:
la oscuridad de un día transcurrido,
de un día alimentado con nuestra triste sangre.

He aquí violetas, golondrinas,
todo cuanto nos gusta y aparece
en las dulces tarjetas de larga cola
por donde se pasean el tiempo y la dulzura.

THERE IS NO FORGETFULNESS
(*Sonata*)

If you ask where I have been
I have to say, "It so happens . . ."
I have to talk about the earth turned dark with stones,
and the river which ruins itself by keeping alive;
I only know about objects that birds lose,
the sea far behind us, or my sister crying.
Why so many different places, why does one day
merge with another day? Why does a black night
gather in the mouth? Why all these people dead?

If you ask where I come from I have to start talking with
        broken objects,
with kitchenware that has too much bitterness,
with animals quite often rotten,
and with my heavy soul.

What have met and crossed are not memories,
nor the yellow pigeon that sleeps in forgetfulness;
but they are faces with tears,
fingers at the throat,
anything that drops out of the leaves:
the shadowiness of a day already passed by,
of a day fed with our own mournful blood.

Look and see violets, swallows,
all those things we love so much and can see
on the tender greeting-cards with long tails
where time and sweetness are sauntering.

Pero no penetremos más allá de esos dientes,
no mordamos las cáscaras que el silencio acumula,
porque no sé qué contestar:
hay tantos muertos,
y tantos malecones que el sol rojo partía,
y tantas cabezas que golpean los buques,
y tantas manos que han encerrado besos,
y tantas cosas que quiero olvidar.

But let's not go deeper than those teeth,
nor bite into the rinds growing over the silence,
because I don't know what to say:
there are so many people dead
and so many sea-walls that the red sun used to split,
and so many heads that the boats hit,
and so many hands that have closed around kisses,
and so many things I would like to forget.

Translated by Robert Bly

from

Tercera Residencia

1935–1945

BRUSELAS

De todo lo que he hecho, de todo lo que he perdido,
de todo lo que he ganado sobresaltadamente,
en hierro amargo, en hojas, puedo ofrecer un poco.
Un sabor asustado, un río que las plumas
de las quemantes águilas van cubriendo, un sulfúrico
retroceso de pétalos.

        No me perdona ya la sal entera
ni el pan continuo, ni la pequeña iglesia devorada
por la lluvia marina, ni el carbón mordido
por la espuma secreta.

He buscado y hallado, pesadamente,
bajo la tierra, entre los cuerpos temibles,
como un diente de pálida madera
llegando y yendo bajo el ácido duro,
junto a los materiales
de la agonía, entre luna y cuchillos,
muriendo de nocturno.

        Ahora, en medio
de la velocidad desestimada, al lado
de los muros sin hilos,
en el fondo cortado por los términos,
aquí estoy con aquello que pierde estrellas,
vegetalmente, solo.

BRUSSELS

Out of everything I've done, everything I've lost,
everything I have gotten unexpectedly,
I can give you a little in leaves, in sour iron.
A terrified flavor, a river that the feathers
of the burning eagles are covering, a sulphurous
retreat of petals.

The undivided salt doesn't forgive me now,
nor the constant bread, nor the tiny church eaten
by the ocean rain, nor the coal bitten
by the secret foam.

I have looked and found, heavily,
under the earth, among the frightening bodies,
like a tooth made of whitish wood,
coming and going under the stubborn acid,
close to the substances
of agony, between moon and knives,
dying at night.

Now in the center
of this speed no one takes seriously, alongside
walls that have no threads,
deep inside cut off at the ends,
here I am with the thing that loses stars,
like a vegetable, alone.

Translated by Robert Bly

from

Canto General

1950

ALGUNAS BESTIAS

Era el crepúsculo de la iguana.
Desde la arcoirisada crestería
su lengua como un dardo
se hundía en la verdura,
el hormiguero monacal pisaba
con melodioso pie la selva,
el guanaco fino como el oxígeno
en las anchas alturas pardas
iba calzando botas de oro,
mientras la llama abría cándidos
ojos en la delicadeza
del mundo lleno de rocío.
Los monos trenzaban un hilo
interminablemente erótico
en las riberas de la aurora,
derribando muros de polen
y espantando el vuelo violeta
de las mariposas de Muzo.
Era la noche de los caimanes,
la noche pura y pululante
de hocicos saliendo del légamo,
y de las ciénagas soñolientas
un ruido opaco de armaduras
volvía al origen terrestre.

El jaguar tocaba las hojas
con su ausencia fosforescente,
el puma corre en el ramaje
como el fuego devorador
mientras arden en él los ojos

SOME BEASTS

It was the twilight of the iguana.
From the rainbow-arch of the battlements,
his long tongue like a lance
sank down in the green leaves,
and a swarm of ants, monks with feet chanting,
crawled off into the jungle,
the guanaco, thin as oxygen
in the wide peaks of cloud,
went along, wearing his shoes of gold,
while the llama opened his honest eyes
on the breakable neatness
of a world full of dew.
The monkeys braided a sexual
thread that went on and on
along the shores of the dawn,
demolishing walls of pollen
and startling the butterflies of Muzo
into flying violets.
It was the night of the alligators,
the pure night, crawling
with snouts emerging from ooze,
and out of the sleepy marshes
the confused noise of scaly plates
returned to the ground where they began.

The jaguar brushed the leaves
with a luminous absence,
the puma runs through the branches
like a forest fire,
while the jungle's drunken eyes

alcohólicos de la selva.
Los tejones rascan los pies
del río, husmean el nido
cuya delicia palpitante
atacarán con dientes rojos.

Y en el fondo del agua magna,
como el círculo de la tierra,
está la gigante anaconda
cubierta de barros rituales,
devoradora y religiosa.

PART I describes South America before the Europeans arrived: the plants and trees, birds, rivers, and minerals, and the Aztec priests coming down the temple stairs looking like "brilliant pheasants." There are eleven poems in this section; we have chosen the second poem, about the animals.

burn from inside him.
The badgers scratch the river's
feet, scenting the nest
whose throbbing delicacy
they attack with red teeth.

And deep in the huge waters
the enormous anaconda lies
like the circle around the earth,
covered with ceremonies of mud,
devouring, religious.

Translated by James Wright

El ser como el maíz se desgranaba en el inacabable
granero de los hechos perdidos, de los acontecimientos
miserables, del uno al siete, al ocho,
y no una muerte, sino muchas muertes llegaba a cada uno:
cada día una muerte pequeña, polvo, gusano, lámpara
que se apaga en el lodo del suburbio, una pequeña muerte
    de alas gruesas
entraba en cada hombre como una corta lanza
y era el hombre asediado del pan o del cuchillo,
el ganadero: el hijo de los puertos, o el capitán oscuro
    del arado,
o el roedor de las calles espesas:

todos desfallecieron esperando su muerte, su corta muerte
    diaria:
y su quebranto aciago de cada día era
como una copa negra que bebían temblando.

PART II, called The Heights of Macchu Picchu is made up of twelve
poems suggested by a visit Neruda made in 1943 to the old ruins of
Macchu Picchu, high in the Andes.

THE HEIGHTS OF MACCHU PICCHU, III

The human soul was threshed out like maize in the endless
granary of defeated actions, of mean things that
 happened,
to the very edge of endurance, and beyond,
and not only death, but many deaths, came to each one:
each day a tiny death, dust, worm, a light
flicked off in the mud at the city's edge, a tiny death with
 coarse wings
pierced into each man like a short lance
and the man was besieged by the bread or by the knife,
the cattle-dealer: the child of sea-harbors, or the dark
 captain of the plough,
or the rag-picker of snarled streets:

everybody lost heart, anxiously waiting for death, the
 short death of every day:
and the grinding bad luck of every day was
like a black cup that they drank, with their hands
 shaking.

Translated by James Wright

LA CABEZA EN EL PALO

Balboa, muerte y garra
llevaste a los rincones de la dulce
tierra central, y entre los perros
cazadores, el tuyo era tu alma:
Leoncico de belfo sangriento
recogió al esclavo que huía,
hundió colmillos españoles
en las gargantas palpitantes,
y de las uñas de los perros
salía la carne al martirio
y la alhaja caía en la bolsa.

Maldito sean perro y hombre,
el aullido infame en la selva
original, el acechante
paso del hierro y del bandido.
Maldita sea la espinosa
corona de la zarza agreste
que no saltó como un erizo
a defender la cuna invadida.

Pero entre los capitanes
sanguinarios se alzó en la sombra
la justicia de los puñales,
la acerba rama de la envidia.

Y al regreso estaba en medio
de tu camino el apellido
de Pedrarias como una soga.

THE HEAD ON THE POLE

Balboa, you brought death and claws
everywhere into the sweet land
of Central America, and among those hunting dogs
your dog was your soul:
with his bloodstained jowls Lioncub
picked up the slave escaping,
sank his Spanish teeth
into the panting throats;
pieces of flesh slipped from
the dogs' jaws into martyrdom
and the jewel fell in the pocket.

A curse on dog and man,
the horrible howl in the unbroken
forest, and the stealthy
walk of the iron and the bandit.
And a curse on the spiny crown
of the wild thornbush
that did not leap like a hedgehog
to protect the invaded cradle.

But the justice of knives,
the bitter branch of envy,
rose in the darkness
among the bloody captains.

And when you got back, the man
named Pedrarias stood
in your way like a rope.

Te juzgaron entre ladridos
de perros matadores de indios.
Ahora que mueres, oyes
el silencio puro, partido
por tus lebreles azuzados?
Ahora que mueres en las manos
de los torvos adelantados,
sientes el aroma dorado
del dulce reino destruído?

Cuando cortaron la cabeza
de Balboa, quedó ensartada
en un palo. Sus ojos muertos
descompusieron su relámpago
y descendieron por la lanza
en un goterón de inmundicia
que desapareció en la tierra.

PART III turns to the European discoverers of South America, and the
conquistadors. One poem describes Columbus' first arrival in 1493, and
his later arrival at Mexico in 1519. Cortez, Balboa, and Ximenez de
Quesada have their own poems; Neruda describes the death of
Atahualpa, and the careers of Valdivia and Magellan. The picture he
gives of these men is often very different from the images of them in
American history books. There are thirty-three poems. We have trans-
lated three, the poems on the fall and death of Balboa, on the death of
Atahualpa, and on Almagro, the discoverer of Chile.

They tried you surrounded by the barkings
of dogs that killed Indians.
Now you are dying, do you hear
the pure silence, broken
by your excited dogs?
Now you are dying in the hands
of the stern authorities,
do you sense the precious aroma
of the sweet kingdom smashed forever?

When they cut off Balboa's
head, it was stuck up
on a pole. His dead eyes
let their lightning rot
and descended along the pole
as a large drop of filth
which disappeared into the earth.

Translated by Robert Bly

LAS AGONÍAS

En Cajamarca empezó la agonía.

El joven Atahualpa, estambre azul,
árbol insigne, escuchó al viento
traer rumor de acero.
Era un confuso
brillo y temblor desde la costa,
un galope increíble
—piafar y poderío—
de hierro y hierro entre la hierba.
Llegaron los adelantados.
El Inca salió de la música
rodeado por los señores.

Las visitas
de otro planeta, sudadas y barbudas,
iban a hacer la reverencia.
El capellán
Valverde, corazón traidor, chacal podrido,
adelanta un extraño objeto, un trozo
de cesto, un fruto
tal vez de aquel planeta
de donde vienen los caballos.
Atahualpa lo toma. No conoce
de qué se trata: no brilla, no suena,
y lo deja caer sonriendo.

"Muerte,
venganza, matad, que os absuelvo",
grita el chacal de la cruz asesina.
El trueno acude hacia los bandoleros.
Nuestra sangre en su cuna es derramada.

ANGUISH OF DEATH

In Cajamarca, the anguish of death began.

The youthful Atahualpa, sky-blue stamen,
illustrious tree, listened to the wind
carry the faint murmur of steel.
There was a confused
light, an earth-tremor from the coast,
an unbelievable galloping—
rearing and power—
from iron and iron, among the weeds.
The governors were arriving.
The Inca came out to the music
surrounded by his nobles.

The visitors
from another planet, sweaty and bearded,
go to do reverence.
The chaplain,
Valverde, treacherous heart, rotten jackal,
brings forward a strange object, a piece
of a basket, a fruit,
perhaps from the same planet from which the horses come.
Atahualpa takes it. He does not know
what it is made of; it doesn't shine, it makes no noise,
and he lets it fall, smiling.

"Death;
vengeance, kill, I will absolve you,"
the jackal of the murderous cross cries out.
Thunder draws near the robbers.
Our blood is shed in its cradle.

Los príncipes rodean como un coro
al Inca, en la hora agonizante.

Diez mil peruanos caen
bajo cruces y espadas, la sangre
moja las vestiduras de Atahualpa.
Pizarro, el cerdo cruel de Extremadura
hace amarrar los delicados brazos
del Inca. La noche ha descendido
sobre el Perú como una brasa negra.

The young princes gather like a chorus
around the Inca, in the hour of the anguish of death.

Ten thousand Peruvians fell
under crosses and swords, the blood
moistened the robes of Atahualpa.
Pizarro, the cruel hog from western Spain,
had the slender arms of the Inca
tied up. Night has now come down
over Peru like a live coal that is black.

Translated by James Wright

DESCUBRIDORES DE CHILE

Del Norte trajo Almagro su arrugada centella.
Y sobre el territorio, entre explosión y ocaso,
se inclinó día y noche como sobre una carta.
Sombra de espinas, sombra de cardo y cera,
el español reunido con su seca figura,
mirando las sombrías estrategias del suelo.
Noche, nieve y arena hacen la forma
de mi delgada patria,
todo el silencio está en su larga línea,
toda la espuma sale de su barba marina,
todo el carbón la llena de misteriosos besos.
Como una brasa el oro arde en sus dedos
y la plata ilumina como una luna verde
su endurecida forma de tétrico planeta.
El español sentado junto a la rosa un día,
junto al aceite, junto al vino, junto al antiguo cielo
no imaginó este punto de colérica piedra
nacer bajo el estiércol del águila marina.

DISCOVERERS OF CHILE

Almagro brought his wrinkled lightning down from the
    north,
and day and night he bent over this country
between gunshots and twilight, as if over a letter.
Shadow of thorn, shadow of thistle and of wax,
the Spaniard, alone with his dried-up body,
watching the shadowy tactics of the soil.
My slim nation has a body made up
of night, snow, and sand,
the silence of the world is in its long coast,
the foam of the world rises from its seaboard,
the coal of the world fills it with mysterious kisses.
Gold burns in its finger like a live coal
and silver lights up like a green moon
its petrified shadow that's like a gloomy planet.
The Spaniard, sitting one day near a rose,
near oil, near wine, near the primitive sky,
could not really grasp how this spot of furious stone
was born beneath the droppings of the ocean eagle.

Translated by Robert Bly

PART IV, called "The Liberators" is the longest section in the book, with
over fifty poems. It concentrates on the liberations in the various
South American countries from the European nations that had col-
onized them. We have chosen the twenty-eighth poem, on the liberator
of Haiti, Toussaint L'Ouverture. There are fine poems also on
  O'Higgins, Lautaro, San Martin, Bolivar, José Marti, and others.

TOUSSAINT L'OUVERTURE

Haití de su dulzura enmarañada,
extrae pétalos patéticos,
rectitud de jardines, edificios
de la grandeza, arrulla
el mar como un abuelo oscuro
su antigua dignidad de piel y espacio.

Toussaint L'Ouverture anuda
la vegetal soberanía,
la majestad encadenada,
la sorda voz de los tambores,
y ataca, cierra el paso, sube,
ordena, expulsa, desafía
como un monarca natural,
hasta que en la red tenebrosa
cae y lo llevan por los mares
arrastrado y atropellado
como el regreso de su raza,
tirado a la muerte secreta
de las sentinas y los sótanos.
Pero en la Isla arden las peñas,
hablan las ramas escondidas,
se trasmiten las esperanzas,
surgen los muros del baluarte.
La libertad es bosque tuyo,
oscuro hermano, preserva
tu memoria de sufrimientos
y que los héroes pasados
custodien tu mágica espuma.

TOUSSAINT L'OUVERTURE

Out of its own tangled sweetness
Haiti raises mournful petals,
and elaborate gardens, magnificent
structures, and rocks the sea
as a dark grandfather rocks
his ancient dignity of skin and space.

Toussaint L'Ouverture knits together
the vegetable kingdom,
the majesty chained,
the monotonous voice of the drums
and attacks, cuts off retreats, rises,
orders, expels, defies
like a natural monarch,
until he falls into the shadowy net
and they carry him over the seas,
dragged along and trampled down
like the return of his race,
thrown into the secret death
of the ship-holds and the cellars.
But on the island the boulders burn,
the hidden branches speak,
hopes are passed on,
the walls of the fortress rise.
Liberty is your own forest,
dark brother, don't lose
the memory of your sufferings,
may the ancestral heroes
have your magic sea-foam in their keeping.

Translated by James Wright

83

LA UNITED FRUIT CO.

Cuando sonó la trompeta, estuvo
todo preparado en la tierra,
y Jehová repartió el mundo
a Coca-Cola Inc., Anaconda,
Ford Motors, y otras entidades:
la Compañía Frutera Inc.
se reservó lo más jugoso,
la costa central de mi tierra,
la dulce cintura de América.
Bautizó de nuevo sus tierras
como "Repúblicas Bananas,"
y sobre los muertos dormidos,
sobre los héroes inquietos
que conquistaron la grandeza,
la libertad y las banderas,
estableció la ópera bufa:
enajenó los albedríos
regaló coronas de César,
desenvainó la envidia, atrajo
la dictadura de las moscas,
moscas Trujillos, moscas Tachos,
moscas Carías, moscas Martínez,
moscas Ubico, moscas húmedas
de sangre humilde y mermelada,
moscas borrachas que zumban
sobre las tumbas populares,
moscas de circo, sabias moscas
entendidas en tiranía.

THE UNITED FRUIT CO.

When the trumpet sounded, it was
all prepared on the earth,
and Jehovah parceled out the earth
to Coca-Cola, Inc., Anaconda,
Ford Motors, and other entities:
The Fruit Company, Inc.
reserved for itself the most succulent,
the central coast of my own land,
the delicate waist of America.
It rechristened its territories
as the "Banana Republics"
and over the sleeping dead,
over the restless heroes
who brought about the greatness,
the liberty and the flags,
it established the comic opera:
abolished the independencies,
presented crowns of Caesar,
unsheathed envy, attracted
the dictatorship of the flies,
Trujillo flies, Tacho flies,
Carias flies, Martinez flies,
Ubico flies, damp flies
of modest blood and marmalade,
drunken flies who zoom
over the ordinary graves,
circus flies, wise flies
well trained in tyranny.

Entre las moscas sanguinarias
la Frutera desembarca,
arrasando el café y las frutas,
en sus barcos que deslizaron
como bandejas el tesoro
de nuestras tierras sumergidas.

Mientras tanto, por los abismos
azucarados de los puertos,
caían indios sepultados
en el vapor de la mañana:
un cuerpo rueda, una cosa
sin nombre, un número caído,
un racimo de fruta muerta
derramada en el pudridero.

PART v, "The Betrayed Sand," concentrates on the men who allowed
South American nations to fall back to colonialism, this time to the
financial colonialism of the United States, and on the men who support
United States' interests today. He mentions the pressure from U.S.
companies to keep wages low. He describes especially events in the
year 1946, while he was a Senator in Chile. We have chosen one of the
poems in the center of the section, on the United Fruit Company.

Among the bloodthirsty flies
the Fruit Company lands its ships,
taking off the coffee and the fruit;
the treasure of our submerged
territories flows as though
on plates into the ships.

Meanwhile Indians are falling
into the sugared chasms
of the harbors, wrapped
for burial in the mist of the dawn:
a body rolls, a thing
that has no name, a fallen cipher,
a cluster of dead fruit
thrown down on the dump.

Translated by Robert Bly

HAMBRE EN EL SUR

Veo el sollozo en el carbón de Lota
y la arrugada sombra del chileno humillado
picar la amarga veta de la entraña, morir,
vivir, nacer en la dura ceniza
agachados, caídos como si el mundo
entrara así y saliera así
entre polvo negro, entre llamas,
y sólo sucediera
la tos en el invierno, el paso
de un caballo en el agua negra, donde ha caído
una hoja de eucaliptus como un cuchillo muerto.

PART VI, called "America, I Do Not Call Your Name Without Hope," is
made of eighteen curious and oblique poems. The long flowing narra-
tives we have become used to in *Canto General* disappear, and we find
instead sudden instants the poem holds back in order to look deep into
them. The language is resonant and fragrant. The poems describe an
instant on horseback in winter, an instant aware of hunger in the coal
mines, an instant aware of the mad frustration of Central America, a
meeting with some seamen in Valparaiso, an instant in Patagonia with
the seals. We have translated four of the poems, including his famous
poem on adolescence, the title poem, a poem on hunger, and "Dicta-
tors," with its powerful, oblique language describing the mood of a
Latin American country under a dictator.

HUNGER IN THE SOUTH

I see the sobbing in the coal at Lota
and the wrinkled shadow of the beaten-down Chilean
pick away at the bitter vein in the core, die,
live, be born in the petrified cinder
bent over, fallen as if the world
could arrive like that or leave like that
among black dust, among flames,
and all that would come out of it would be
the cough in winter, the step
of a horse in the black water, where
a eucalyptus leaf has fallen like a dead knife.

Translated by Robert Bly

JUVENTUD

Un perfume como una ácida espada
de ciruelas en un camino,
los besos del azúcar en los dientes,
las gotas vitales resbalando en los dedos,
la dulce pulpa erótica,
las eras, los pajares, los incitantes
sitios secretos de las casas anchas,
los colchones dormidos en el pasado, el agrio valle verde
mirado desde arriba, desde el vidrio escondido:
toda la adolescencia mojándose y ardiendo
como una lámpara derribada en la lluvia.

YOUTH

An odor like an acid sword made
of plum branches along the road,
the kisses like sugar in the teeth,
the drops of life slipping on the fingertips,
the sweet sexual fruit,
the yards, the haystacks, the inviting
rooms hidden in the deep houses,
the mattresses sleeping in the past, the savage green
    valley
seen from above, from the hidden window:
adolescence all sputtering and burning
like a lamp turned over in the rain.

Translated by Robert Bly

LOS DICTADORES

Ha quedado un olor entre los cañaverales:
una mezcla de sangre y cuerpo, un penetrante
pétalo nauseabundo.
Entre los cocoteros las tumbas están !lenas
de huesos demolidos, de estertores callados.
El delicado sátrapa conversa
con copas, cuellos y cordones de oro.
El pequeño palacio brilla como un reloj
y las rápidas risas enguantadas
atraviesan a veces los pasillos
y se reúnen a las voces muertas
y a las bocas azules frescamente enterradas.
El llanto está escondido como una planta
cuya semilla cae sin cesar sobre el suelo
y hace crecer sin luz sus grandes hojas ciegas.
El odio se ha formado escama a escama,
golpe a golpe, en el agua terrible del pantano,
con un hocico lleno de légamo y silencio.

THE DICTATORS

An odor has remained among the sugarcane:
a mixture of blood and body, a penetrating
petal that brings nausea.
Between the coconut palms the graves are full
of ruined bones, of speechless death-rattles.
The delicate dictator is talking
with top hats, gold braid, and collars.
The tiny palace gleams like a watch
and the rapid laughs with gloves on
cross the corridors at times
and join the dead voices
and the blue mouths freshly buried.
The weeping cannot be seen, like a plant
whose seeds fall endlessly on the earth,
whose large blind leaves grow even without light.
Hatred has grown scale on scale,
blow on blow, in the ghastly water of the swamp,
with a snout full of ooze and silence.

Translated by Robert Bly

93

AMÉRICA, NO INVOCO TU NOMBRE EN VANO

América, no invoco tu nombre en vano.
Cuando sujeto al corazón la espada,
cuando aguanto en el alma la gotera,
cuando por las ventanas
un nuevo día tuyo me penetra,
soy y estoy en la luz que me produce,
vivo en la sombra que me determina,
duermo y despierto en tu esencial aurora:
dulce como las uvas, y terrible,
conductor del azúcar y el castigo,
empapado en esperma de tu especie,
amamantado en sangre de tu herencia.

AMERICA, I DO NOT CALL
YOUR NAME WITHOUT HOPE

America, I do not call your name without hope.
When I hold the sword against the heart,
when I live with the faulty roof in the soul,
when one of your new days
pierces me coming through the windows,
I am and I stand in the light that produces me,
I live in the darkness which makes me what I am,
I sleep and awake in your fundamental sunrise:
as mild as the grapes, and as terrible,
carrier of sugar and the whip,
soaked in the sperm of your species,
nursed on the blood of your inheritance.

Translated by Robert Bly

HIMNO Y REGRESO (1939)

Patria, mi patria, vuelvo hacia ti la sangre.
Pero te pido, como a la madre el niño
lleno de llanto.
        Acoge
esta guitarra ciega
y esta frente perdida.
Salí a encontrarte hijos por la tierra,
salí a cuidar caídos con tu nombre de nieve,
salí a hacer una casa con tu madera pura,
salí a llevar tu estrella a los héroes heridos.

Ahora quiero dormir en tu substancia.
Dame tu clara noche de penetrantes cuerdas,
tu noche de navío, tu estatura estrellada.

Patria mía: quiero mudar de sombra.
Patria mía: quiero cambiar de rosa.
Quiero poner mi brazo en tu cintura exigua
y sentarme en tus piedras por el mar calcinadas,
a detener el trigo y mirarlo por dentro.
Voy a escoger la flora delgada del nitrato,
voy a hilar el estambre glacial de la campaña,
y mirando tu ilustre y solitaria espuma
un ramo litoral tejeré a tu belleza.

Patria, mi patria
toda rodeada de agua combatiente
y nieve combatida,
en ti se junta el águila al azufre,

HYMN AND RETURN

(1939)

Country, my country, I turn my blood in your direction.
But I am begging you the way a child begs its mother,
with tears:
           take this blind guitar
and these lost features.
I left to find sons for you over the earth,
I left to comfort those fallen with your name made of
      snow,
I left to build a house with your pure timber,
I left to carry your star to the wounded heroes.

Now I want to fall asleep in your substance.
Give me your clear night of piercing strings,
your night like a ship, your altitude covered with stars.

My country: I want to change my shadow.
My country: I want to have another rose.
I want to put my arm around your narrow waist
and sit down on your stones whitened by the sea
and hold the wheat back and look deep into it.
I am going to pick the thin flower of nitrate,
I am going to feel the icy wool of the field,
and staring at your famous and lonesome sea-foam
I'll weave with them a wreath on the shore for your
      beauty.

Country, my country,
entirely surrounded by aggressive water
and fighting snow,
the eagle and the sulphur come together in you,

97

y en tu antártica mano de armiño y de zafiro
una gota de pura luz humana
brilla encendiendo el enemigo cielo.

Guarda tu luz, oh patria !, mantén
tu dura espiga de esperanza en medio
del ciego aire temible.
En tu remota tierra ha caído toda esta luz difícil,
este destino de los hombres,
que te hace defender una flor misteriosa
sola, en la inmensidad de América dormida.

PART VII, called "Canto General of Chile," was evidently the seed of
the whole book, and contains some of the earliest poems written for
the volume. Neruda touches on the geography and history of Chile
here in a way he was later to do for all of South America. It is a
sort of ode of praise to Chile, a homesick poem. The poem "Ocean,"
often translated, is from this section. We have chosen the poem he
wrote in 1939, after deciding to go back to Chile following the collapse
of the Spanish Republican army, a poem called "Hymn and Return."

and a drop of pure human light
burns in your antarctic hand of ermine and sapphire,
lighting up the hostile sky.

My country, take care of your light! Hold up
your stiff straw of hope
into the blind and frightening air.
All of this difficult light has fallen on your isolated land,
this future of the race,
that makes you defend a mysterious flower
alone, in the hugeness of an America that lies asleep.

Translated by Robert Bly

The poems in PART VIII are centered about people, usually ordinary or
"unknown" Chileans. At times the Chileans themselves talk, telling
their stories, at other times Neruda describes their lives. Several of
the monologues contain descriptions of torture performed by the police.
The poems vary in quality. We have chosen the first poem of the four-
teen, about a shoveler Neruda met in the nitrate works.

CRISTÓBAL MIRANDA

(Palero-Tocopilla)

Te conocí, Cristóbal, en las lanchas anchas
de la bahía, cuando baja
el salitre, hacia el mar, en la quemante
vestidura de un día de Noviembre.
Recuerdo aquella extática apostura,
los cerros de metal, el agua quieta.
Y sólo el hombre de las lanchas, húmedo
de sudor, moviendo nieve.
Nieve de los nitratos, derramada
sobre los hombros del dolor, cayendo
a la barriga ciega de las naves.
Allí, paleros, héroes de una aurora
carcomida por ácidos, sujeta
a los destinos de la muerte, firmes,
recibiendo el nitrato caudaloso.
Cristóbal, este recuerdo para ti.
Para los camaradas de la pala,
a cuyos pechos entra el ácido
y las emanaciones asesinas,
hinchando como águilas aplastadas
los corazones, hasta que cae el hombre,
hasta que rueda el hombre hacia las calles,
hacia las cruces rotas de la pampa.
Bien, no digamos más, Cristóbal, ahora
este papel que te recuerda, a todos,
a los lancheros de bahía, al hombre
ennegrecido de los barcos, mis ojos

CRISTOBAL MIRANDA

(Shoveler at Tocopilla)

I met you on the broad barges
in the bay, Cristobal, while the sodium nitrate
was coming down, wrapped in a burning
November day, to the sea.
I remember the ecstatic nimbleness,
the hills of metal, the motionless water.
And only the bargemen, soaked
with sweat, moving snow.
Snow of the nitrates, poured
over painful shoulders, dropping
into the blind stomach of the ships.
Shovelers there, heroes of a sunrise
eaten away by acids, and bound
to the destinies of death, standing firm,
taking in the floods of nitrate.
Cristobal, this memento is for you,
for the others shoveling with you,
whose chests are penetrated by the acids
and the lethal gases,
making the heart swell up
like crushed eagles, until the man drops,
rolls toward the streets of town,
toward the broken crosses out in the field.
Enough of that, Cristobal, today
this bit of paper remembers you, each of you,
the bargemen of the bay, the man
turned black in the boats, my eyes

van con vosotros en esta jornada
y mi alma es una pala que levanta
cargando y descargando sangre y nieve,
junto a vosotros, vidas del desierto.

are moving with yours in this daily work
and my soul is a shovel which lifts
loading and unloading blood and snow
next to you, creatures of the desert.

Translated by Robert Bly

QUE DESPIERTE EL LEÑADOR

Al oeste de Colorado River
hay un sitio que amo.
Acudo allí con todo lo que palpitando
transcurre en mí, con todo
lo que fuí, lo que soy, lo que sostengo.
Hay unas altas piedras rojas, el aire
salvaje de mil manos
las hizo edificadas estructuras:
el escarlata ciego subió desde el abismo
y en ellas se hizo cobre, fuego y fuerza.
América extendida como la piel de búfalo,
aérea y clara noche del galope,
allí hacia las alturas estrelladas,
bebo tu copa de verde rocío.

Sí, por agria Arizona y Wisconsin nudoso,
hasta Milwaukee levantada contra el viento y la nieve
o en los enardecidos pantanos de West Palm,
cerca de los pinares de Tacoma, en el espeso
olor de acero de tus bosques,
anduve pisando tierra madre,
hojas azules, piedras de cascada,
huracanes que temblaban como toda la música,
ríos que rezaban como los monasterios,
ánades y manzanas, tierras y aguas,
infinita quietud para que el trigo nazca.

Allí pude, en mi piedra central, etender al aire
ojos, oídos, manos, hasta oír

I WISH THE WOODCUTTER
WOULD WAKE UP

West of the Colorado River
there's a place I love.
I take refuge there with everything alive
in me, with everything
that I have been, that I am, that I believe in.
Some high red rocks are there, the wild
air with its thousand hands
has turned them into human buildings.
The blind scarlet rose from the depths
and changed in these rocks to copper, fire, and energy.
America spread out like a buffalo skin,
light and transparent night of galloping,
near your high places covered with stars
I drink down your cup of green dew.

Yes, through acrid Arizona and Wisconsin full of knots,
as far as Milwaukee, raised to keep back the wind and the
        snow
or in the burning swamps of West Palm,
near the pine trees of Tacoma, in the thick odor
of your forests which is like steel,
I walked weighing down the mother earth,
blue leaves, waterfalls of stones,
hurricanes vibrating as all music does,
rivers that muttered prayers like monasteries,
geese and apples, territories and waters,
infinite silence in which the wheat could be born.

I was able there, in my deep stony core, to stretch my
        eyes, ears, hands,
far out into the air until I heard

libros, locomotoras, nieve, luchas,
fábricas, tumbas, vegetales, pasos,
y de Manhattan la luna en el navío,
el canto de la máquina que hila,
la cuchara de hierro que come tierra,
la perforadora con su golpe de cóndor
y cuanto corta, oprime, corre, cose:
seres y ruedas repitiendo y naciendo.

Amo el pequeño hogar del *farmer*. Recientes madres
    duermen
aromadas como el jarabe del tamarindo, las telas
recién planchadas. Arde
el fuego de mil hogares rodeados de cebollas.
(Los hombres cuando cantan cerca del río tienen
una voz ronca como las piedras del fondo:
el tabaco salió de sus anchas hojas
y como un duende del fuego llegó a estos hogares.)
Missouri adentro venid, mirad el queso y la harina,
las tablas olorosas, rojas como violines,
el hombre navegando la cebada,
el potro azul recién montado huele
el aroma del pan y de la alfalfa:
campanas, amapolas, herrerías,
y en los destartalados cinemas silvestres
el amor abre su dentadura
en el sueño nacido de la tierra.
Es tu paz lo que amamos, no tu máscara.
No es hermoso tu rostro de guerrero.
Eres hermosa y ancha Norte América.
Vienes de humilde cuna como una lavandera,
junto a tus ríos, blanca.
Edificada en lo desconocido,
es tu paz de panal lo dulce tuyo.

books, locomotives, snow, battles,
factories, cemeteries, footsteps, plants,
and the moon on a ship from Manhattan,
the song of the machine that is weaving,
the iron spoon that eats the earth,
the drill that strikes like a condor,
and everything that cuts, presses, sews:
creatures and wheels repeating themselves and being
      born.

I love the farmer's small house. New mothers are asleep
with a good smell like the sap of the tamarind, clothes
just ironed. Fires are burning in a thousand homes,
with drying onions hanging around the fireplace.
(When they are singing near the river the men's voices
are deep as the stones at the river bottom;
and tobacco rose from its wide leaves
and entered these houses like a spirit of the fire.)
Come deeper into Missouri, look at the cheese and the
      flour,
the boards aromatic and red as violins,
the man moving like a ship among the barley,
the blue-black colt just home from a ride smells
the odor of bread and alfalfa:
bells, poppies, blacksmith shops,
and in the rundown movies in the small towns
love opens its mouth full of teeth
in a dream born of the earth.
What we love is your peace, not your mask.
Your warrior's face is not handsome.
North America, you are handsome and spacious.
You come, like a washerwoman, from
a simple cradle, near your rivers, pale.
Built up from the unknown,
what is sweet in you is your hivelike peace.

Amanos tu hombre con las manos rojas
de barro de Oregón, tu niño negro
que te trajo la música nacida
en su comarca de marfil: amamos
tu ciudad, tu substancia,
tu luz, tus mecanismos, la energía
del Oeste, la pacífica
miel, de colmenar y aldea,
el gigante muchacho en el tractor,
la avena que heredaste
de Jefferson, la rueda rumorosa
que mide tu terrestre oceanía,
el humo de una fábrica y el beso
número mil de una colonia nueva:
tu sangre labradora es la que amamos:
tu mano popular llena de aceite.

Bajo la noche de las praderas hace ya tiempo
reposan sobre la piel del búfalo en un grave
silencio las sílabas, el canto
de lo que fuí antes de ser, de lo que fuimos.
Melville es un abeto marino, de sus ramas
nace una curva de carena, un brazo
de madera y navío. Whitman innumerable
como los cereales, Poe en su matemática
tiniebla, Dreiser, Wolfe,
frescas heridas de nuestra propia ausencia,
Lockridge reciente, atados a la profundidad,
cuántos otros atados a la sombra:
sobre ellos la misma aurora del hemisferio arde
y de ellos está hecho lo que somos.
Poderosos infantes, capitanes ciegos,
entre acontecimientos y follajes amedrentados a veces,

We love the man with his hands red
from the Oregon clay, your Negro boy
who brought you the music born
in his country of tusks: we love
your city, your substance,
your light, your machines, the energy
of the West, the harmless
honey from hives and little towns,
the huge farmboy on his tractor,
the oats which you inherited
from Jefferson, the noisy wheel
that measures your oceanic earth,
the factory smoke and the kiss,
the thousandth, of a new colony:
what we love is your workingman's blood:
your unpretentious hand covered with oil.

For years now under the prairie night
in a heavy silence on the buffalo skin
syllables have been asleep, poems
about what I was before I was born, what we were.
Melville is a sea fir, the curve of the keel
springs from his branches, an arm
of timber and ship. Whitman impossible to count
as grain, Poe in his mathematical
darkness, Dreiser, Wolfe,
fresh wounds of our own absence,
Lockridge more recently, all bound to the depths,
how many others, bound to the darkness:
over them the same dawn of the hemisphere burns,
and out of them what we are has come.
Powerful foot soldiers, blind captains,
frightened at times among actions and leaves,

interrumpidos por la alegría y por el duelo,
bajo las praderas cruzadas de tráfico,
cuántos muertos en las llanuras antes no visitadas:
inocentes atormentados, profetas recién impresos,
sobre la piel del búfalo de las praderas.

De Francia, de Okinawa, de los atolones
de Leyte (Norman Mailer lo ha dejado escrito),
del aire enfurecido y de las olas,
han regresado casi todos los muchachos.
Casi todos . . . Fué verde y amarga la historia
de barro y sudor: no oyeron
bastante el canto de los arrecifes
ni tocaron tal vez sino para morir en las islas, las coronas
de fulgor y fragancia:
                    sangre y estiércol
los persiguieron, la mugre y las ratas,
y un cansado y desolado corazón que luchaba.
Pero ya han vuelto,
                    los habéis recibido
en el ancho espacio de las tierras extendidas
y se han cerrado (los que han vuelto) como una corola
de innumerables pétalos anónimos
para renacer y olvidar.

(1948)

PART IX returns to a consideration of the United States. It opens with
the vivid poem printed here, and then goes on to ask why it is the
United States is always on the dictators' side, and consistently attempts
to destroy risings anywhere in the world. Neruda warns the United
States not to invade South America, and wishes that "Abraham Lincoln
would wake up." This entire section, translated as "Let the Rail-
splitter Awake" was printed as a pamphlet by *Masses And Main-
stream*. Some of the pieces are crude propaganda, others fresh and
generous poems.

110

checked in their work by joy and by mourning,
under the plains crossed by traffic,
how many dead men in the fields never visited before:
innocent ones tortured, prophets only now published,
on the buffalo skin of the prairies.

From France, and Okinawa, and the atolls
of Leyte (Norman Mailer has written it out)
and the infuriated air and the waves,
almost all the men have come back now,
almost all . . . The history of mud and sweat
was green and sour; they did not hear
the singing of the reefs long enough
and perhaps never touched the islands, those wreaths of
    brilliance and perfume,
except to die:
             dung and blood
hounded them, the filth and the rats,
and a fatigued and ruined heart that went on fighting.
But they have come back,
                you have received them
into the immensity of the open lands
and they have closed (those who came back) like a flower
with thousands of nameless petals
to be reborn and forget.

(1948)

Translated by Robert Bly

"ERA EL OTOÑO DE LAS UVAS"

Era el otoño de las uvas.
Temblaba el parral numeroso.
Los racimos blancos, velados,
escarchaban sus dulces dedos,
y las negras uvas llenaban
sus pequeñas ubres repletas
de un secreto río redondo.
El dueño de casa, artesano
de magro rostro, me leía
el pálido libro terrestre
de los días crepusculares.
Su bondad conocía el fruto,
la rama troncal y el trabajo
de la poda que deja al árbol
su desnuda forma de copa.
A los caballos conversaba
como a inmensos niños: seguían
detrás de él los cinco gatos
y los perros de aquella casa,
unos enarcados y lentos,
otros corriendo locamente
bajo los fríos duraznos.
Él conocía cada rama,
cada cicatriz de los árboles,
y su antigua voz me enseñaba
acariciando a los caballos.

PART x, "The Fugitive" was written during the months Gonzalez
Videla's police were pursuing him. Its thirteen poems describe being
led at night through unlit streets, knocking on the door, and living a
day or two with families that were risking their lives to take him in. It
is a poem of thanks to those who helped him. We chose the second
poem, on a host who had horses.

"IT WAS THE GRAPE'S AUTUMN"

It was the grape's autumn.
The dense vinefield shivered.
The white clusters, half-hidden,
found their mild fingers cold,
and the black grapes were filling
their tiny stout udders
from a round and secret river.
The man of the house, an artisan
with a hawk's face, read to me
the pale earth book
about the darkening days.
His kindliness saw deep into the fruit,
the trunk of the vine, and the work
of the pruning knife, which lets the tree keep
its simple goblet shape.
He talked to his horses
as if to immense boys: behind him
the five cats trailed,
and the dogs of that household,
some arched and slow moving,
others running crazily
under the cold peach trees.
He knew each branch,
each scar on his trees,
and his ancient voice taught me
while it was stroking his horses.

Translated by James Wright
and Robert Bly

LA HUELGA

Extraña era la fábrica inactiva.
Un silencio en la planta, una distancia
entre máquina y hombre, como un hilo
cortado entre planetas, un vacío
de las manos del hombre que consumen
el tiempo construyendo, y las desnudas
estancias sin trabajo y sin sonido.
Cuando el hombre dejó las madrigueras
de la turbina, cuando desprendió
los brazos de la hoguera y decayeron
las entrañas del horno, cuando sacó los ojos
de la rueda y la luz vertiginosa
se detuvo en su círculo invisible,
de todos los poderes poderosos,
de los círculos puros de potencia,
de la energía sobrecogedora,
quedó un montón de inútiles aceros
y en las salas sin hombre, el aire viudo,
el solitario aroma del aceite.

In PART XI, he describes a visit he made to Punitaqui and its gold mine
in 1946, while he was a Senator. It was cactus and boulders and
drought; farmers asking him to speak to "the Ministry," toward pos-
sible help for the starving. We have chosen the thirteenth of the
fifteen poems, describing the mood in a factory during a long strike he
watched there.

THE STRIKE

The idle factory came to seem strange.
A silence in the plant, a distance
between machine and man, as if a thread had been cut
between two planets, an absence
of human hands that use up time
making things, and the naked
rooms without work and without noise.
When man deserted the lairs
of the turbine, when he tore off
the arms of the fire, so that the inner organs
of the furnace died, and pulled out the eyes
of the wheel, so that the dizzy light
paused in its invisible circle,
the eyes of the great energies,
of the pure circles of force,
of the stupendous power,
what remained was a heap of pointless pieces of steel,
and in the shops without men a widowed air
and the lonesome odor of oil.

Nada existía sin aquel fragmento
golpeando, sin Ramírez,
sin el hombre de ropa desgarrada.
Allí estaba la piel de los motores,
acumulada en muerto poderío,
como negros cetáceos en el fondo
pestilente de un mar sin oleaje,
o montañas hundidas de repente
bajo la soledad de los planetas.

Nothing existed without that fragment
hammering, without Ramirez,
without the man in torn overalls.
Nothing was left but the hides of the engines,
heaps of power gone dead,
like black whales in the polluted
depths of a sluggish sea,
or mountain ranges suddenly drowned
under the loneliness of outer space.

Translated by Robert Bly

PART XII is made up of five long poems to friends. All five friends, at
great sacrifice to themselves, had fought against business and the
right wing. Among the friends are Miguel Hernandez and Rafael
Alberti. We have chosen the first, the joyful poem written to the
Venezuelan poet, Miguel Otero Silva. Neruda wrote it while still in
hiding, and he knows the police will try to deduce from the details in
the poem where he is, so he tells Silva many details about seagulls,
"useful to the State." Nicolas Guillen is the Cuban poet, still alive.

CARTA A MIGUEL OTERO SILVA, EN CARACAS

(1948)

Nicolás Guillén me trajo tu carta escrita
con palabras invisibles, sobre su traje, en sus ojos.
Qué alegre eres, Miguel, qué alegres somos!
Ya no queda en un mundo de úlceras estucadas
sino nosotros, indefinidamente alegres.
Veo pasar al cuervo y no me puede hacer daño.
Tú observas el escorpión y limpias tu guitarra.
Vivimos entre las fieras, cantando, y cuando tocamos
un hombre, la materia de alguien en quien creíamos,
y éste se desmorona como un pastel podrido,
tú en tu venezolano patrimonio recoges
lo que puede salvarse, mientras que yo defiendo
la brasa de la vida.
                    Qué alegría, Miguel!
Tú me preguntas dónde estoy? Te contaré
—dando sólo detalles *útiles* al Gobierno—
que en esta costa llena de piedras salvajes
se unen el mar y el campo, olas y pinos,
águilas y petreles, espumas y praderas.
Has visto desde muy cerca y todo el día
cómo vuelan los pájaros del mar? Parece
que llevaran las cartas del mundo a sus destinos.
Pasan los alcatraces como barcos del viento,
otras aves que vuelan como flechas y traen
los mensajes de reyes difuntos, de los príncipes
enterrados con hilos de turquesa en las costas andinas,

LETTER TO MIGUEL OTERO SILVA,
IN CARACAS

(1948)

Nicolas Guillen brought me your letter, written
invisibly, on his clothes, in his eyes.
How happy you are, Miguel, both of us are!
In a world that festering plaster almost covers
there is no one left aimlessly happy but us.
I see the crow go by; there's nothing he can do to harm
    me.
You watch the scorpion, and polish your guitar.
Writing poetry, we live among the wild beasts, and when
    we touch
a man, the stuff of someone in whom we believed,
and he goes to pieces like a rotten pie,
you in the Venezuela you inherited gather together
whatever can be salvaged, while I cup my hands
around the live coal of life.
                    What happiness, Miguel!
Are you going to ask where I am? I'll tell you—
giving only details useful to the State—
that on this coast scattered with wild rocks
the sea and the fields come together, the waves and the
    pines,
petrels and eagles, meadows and foam.
Have you ever spent a whole day close to sea birds,
watching how they fly? They seem
to be carrying the letters of the world to their destina-
    tions.
The pelicans go by like ships of the wind,
other birds go by like arrows, carrying
messages from dead kings, viceroys,
buried with strands of turquoise on the Andean coasts,

y las gaviotas hechas de blancura redonda,
que olvidan continuamente sus mensajes.
Qué azul es la vida, Miguel, cuando hemos puesto en ella
amor y lucha, palabras que son el pan y el vino,
palabras que ellos no pueden deshonrar todavía,
porque nosotros salimos a la calle con escopeta y cantos.
Están perdidos con nosotros, Miguel.
Qué pueden hacer sino matarnos y aun así
les resulta un mal negocio, sólo pueden
tratar de alquilar un piso frente a nosotros y seguirnos
para aprender a reír y a llorar como nosotros.
Cuando yo escribía versos de amor, que me brotaban
por todas partes, y me moría de tristeza,
errante, abandonado, royendo el alfabeto,
me decían: "Qué grande eres, oh Teócrito!"
Yo no soy Teócrito: tomé a la vida,
me puse frente a ella, la besé hasta vencerla,
y luego me fuí por los callejones de las minas
a ver cómo vivían otros hombres.
Y cuando salí con las manos teñidas de basura y dolores,
las levanté mostrándolas en las cuerdas de oro,
y dije: "Yo no comparto el crimen".
Tosieron, se disgustaron mucho, me quitaron el saludo,
me dejaron de llamar Teócrito, y terminaron
por insultarme y mandar toda la policía a encarcelarme,
porque no seguía preocupado exclusivamente de asuntos
    metafísicos.
Pero yo había conquistado la alegría.
Desde entonces me levanté leyendo las cartas
que traen las aves del mar desde tan lejos,

and seagulls, so magnificently white,
they are constantly forgetting what their messages are.
Life is like the sky, Miguel, when we put
loving and fighting in it, words that are bread and wine,
words they have not been able to degrade even now,
because we walk out in the street with poems and guns.
They don't know what to do with us, Miguel.
What can they do but kill us; and even that
wouldn't be a good bargain—nothing they can do
but rent a room across the street, and tail us
so they can learn to laugh and cry like us.
When I was writing my love poems, which sprouted out
        from me
on all sides, and I was dying of depression,
nomadic, abandoned, gnawing on the alphabet,
they said to me: "What a great man you are,
        Theocritus!"
I am not Theocritus: I took life,
and I faced her and kissed her,
and then went through the tunnels of the mines
to see how other men live.
And when I came out, my hands stained with garbage
        and sadness,
I held my hands up and showed them to the generals,
and said: "I am not a part of this crime."
They started to cough, showed disgust, left off saying
        hello,
gave up calling me Theocritus, and ended by insulting
        me
and assigning the entire police force to arrest me
because I didn't continue to be occupied exclusively with
        metaphysical subjects.
But I had brought joy over to my side.
From then on I started getting up to read the letters
the sea birds bring from so far away,

121

cartas que vienen mojadas, mensajes que poco a poco
voy traduciendo con lentitud y seguridad: soy meticuloso
como un ingeniero en este extraño oficio.
Y salgo de repente a la ventana. Es un cuadrado
de transparencia, es pura la distancia
de hierbas y peñascos, y así voy trabajando
entre las cosas que amo: olas, piedras, avispas,
con una embriagadora felicidad marina.
Pero a nadie le gusta que estemos alegres, a ti te
       asignaron
un papel bonachón: "Pero no exagere, no se preocupe",
y a mí me quisieron clavar en un insectario, entre las
       lágrimas,
para que éstas me ahogaran y ellos pudieron decir sus
       discursos en mi tumba.

Yo recuerdo un día en la pampa arenosa
del salitre, había quinientos hombres
en huelga. Era la tarde abrasadora
de Tarapacá. Y cuando los rostros habían recogido
toda la arena y el desangrado sol seco del desierto,
yo vi llegar a mi corazón, como una copa que odio,
la vieja melancolía. Aquella hora de crisis,
en la desolación de los salares, en ese minuto débil de
la lucha, en que podríamos haber sido vencidos,
una niña pequeñita y pálida venida de las minas
dijo con una voz valiente en que se juntaban el cristal y
       el acero
un poema tuyo, un viejo poema tuyo que rueda entre los
       ojos arrugados
de todos los obreros y labradores de mi patria, de
       América.
Y aquel trozo de canto tuyo refulgió de repente
en mi boca como una flor purpúrea
y bajó hacia mi sangre, llenándola de nuevo

letters that arrive moist, messages I translate
phrase by phrase, slowly and confidently: I am punc-
    tilious
as an engineer in this strange duty.
All at once I go to the window. It is a square
of pure light, there is a clear horizon
of grasses and crags, and I go on working here
among the things I love: waves, rocks, wasps,
with an oceanic and drunken happiness.
But no one likes our being happy, and they cast you
in a genial role: "Now don't exaggerate, don't worry,"
and they wanted to lock me in a cricket cage, where there
    would be tears,
and I would drown, and they could deliver elegies over
    my grave.

I remember one day in the sandy acres
of the nitrate flats; there were five hundred men
on strike. It was a scorching afternoon
in Tarapaca. And after the faces had absorbed
all the sand and the bloodless dry sun of the desert,
I saw coming into me, like a cup that I hate,
my old depression. At this time of crisis,
in the desolation of the salt flats, in that weak moment
of the fight, when we could have been beaten,
a little pale girl who had come from the mines
spoke a poem of yours in a brave voice that had glass in it
    and steel,
an old poem of yours that wanders among the wrinkled
    eyes
of all the workers of my country, of America.
And that small piece of your poetry blazed suddenly
like a purple blossom in my mouth,
and went down to my blood, filling it once more

con una alegría desbordante nacida de tu canto.
Y yo pensé no sólo en ti, sino en tu Venezuela amarga.
Hace años, vi un estudiante que tenía en los tobillos
la señal de las cadenas que un general le había impuesto,
y me contó cómo los encadenados trabajaban en los
      caminos
y los calabozos donde la gente se perdía. Porque así ha
      sido nuestra América:
una llanura con ríos devorantes y constelaciones
de mariposas (en algunos sitios, las esmeraldas son
      espesas como manzanas),
pero siempre a lo largo de la noche y de los ríos
hay tobillos que sangran, antes cerca del petróleo,
hoy cerca del nitrato, en Pisagua, donde un déspota sucio
ha enterrado la flor de mi patria para que muera, y él
      pueda comerciar con los huesos.
Por eso cantas, por eso, para que América deshonrada y
      herida
haga temblar sus mariposas y recoja sus esmeraldas
sin la espantosa sangre del castigo, coagulada
en las manos de los verdugos y de los mercaderes.
Yo comprendí qué alegre estarías, cerca del Orinoco,
      cantando,
seguramente, o bien comprando vino para tu casa,
ocupando tu puesto en la lucha y en la alegría,
ancho de hombros, como son los poetas de este tiempo
—con trajes claros y zapatos de camino—.
Desde entonces, he ido pensando que alguna vez te
      escribiría,
y cuando Guillén llegó, todo lleno de historias tuyas
que se le desprendían de todo el traje
y que bajo los castaños de mi casa se derramaron,
me dije: "Ahora", y tampoco comencé a escribirte.

with a luxuriant joy born from your poem.
I thought of you, but also of your bitter Venezuela.
Years ago I saw a student who had marks on his ankles
from chains ordered on him by a general,
and he told me of the chain gangs that work on the roads
and the jails where people disappeared forever. Because
    that is what our America has been:
long stretches with destructive rivers and constellations
of butterflies (in some places the emeralds are heavy as
    apples).
But along the whole length of the night and the rivers
there are always bleeding ankles, at one time near the oil
    wells,
now near the nitrate, in Pisagua, where a rotten leader
has put the best men of my country under the earth to
    die, so he can sell their bones.
That is why you write your songs, so that someday the
    disgraced and wounded America
can let its butterflies tremble and collect its emeralds
without the terrifying blood of beatings, coagulated
on the hands of the executioners and the businessmen.
I guessed how full of joy you would be, by the Orinoco,
    singing
probably, or perhaps buying wine for your house,
taking your part in the fight and the exaltation,
with broad shoulders, like the poets of our age—
with light clothes and walking shoes.
Ever since that time, I have been thinking of writing to
    you,
and when Guillen arrived, running over with stories of
    you,
which were coming loose everywhere out of his clothes
—they poured out under the chestnuts of my house—
I said to myself: "Now!" and even then I didn't start a
    letter to you.

Pero hoy ha sido demasiado: pasó por mi ventana
no sólo un ave del mar, sino millares,
y recogí las cartas que nadie lee y que ellas llevan
por las orillas del mundo, hasta perderlas.
Y entonces, en cada una leía palabras tuyas
y eran como las que yo escribo y sueño y canto,
y entonces decidí enviarte esta carta, que termino aquí
para mirar por la ventana el mundo que nos pertenece.

But today has been too much for me: not only one sea
     bird,
but thousands have gone past my window,
and I have picked up the letters no one reads, letters
     they take along
to all the shores of the world until they lose them.
Then in each of those letters I read words of yours,
and they resembled the words I write, and dream of, and
          put in poems,
and so I decided to send this letter to you, which I end
     here,
so I can watch through the window the world that is ours.

Translated by Robert Bly

PART XIII is a New Year's greeting to Chile, for January 1, 1949, written
after Neruda had succeeded in getting over the Andes, and to Europe.
He talks of the many South American countries still under dictator-
ship, "dancing with the sharpened teeth of the night-time alligators."
The United States support of these dictators he considers part of a
general foreign policy, policy of an "empire," which destroys client
countries. We chose "They Receive Orders Against Chile."

RECIBEN ÓRDENES CONTRA CHILE

Pero detrás de todos ellos hay que buscar, hay algo
detrás de los traidores y las ratas que roen,
hay un imperio que pone la mesa,
que sirve las comidas y las balas.
Quieren hacer de ti lo que logran en Grecia.
Los señoritos griegos en el banquete, y balas
al pueblo en las montañas: hay que extirpar el vuelo
de la nueva Victoria de Samotracia, hay que ahorcar,
matar, perder, hundir el cuchillo aesino
empuñado en New York, hay que romper con fuego
el orgullo del hombre que asomaba
por todas partes como si naciera
de la tierra regada por la sangre.
Hay que armar a Chiang y al ínfimo Videla,
hay que darles dinero para cárceles, alas
para que bombardeen compatriotas, hay que darles
un mendrugo, unos dólares, ellos hacen el resto,
ellos mienten, corrompen, bailan sobre los muertos
y sus esposas lucen los "visones" más caros.
No importa la agonía del pueblo, este martirio
necesitan los amos dueños del cobre: hay hechos:
los generales dejan el ejército y sirven
de asistentes al Staff en Chuquicamata,
y en el salitre el general "chileno"
manda con su charrasca cuánto deben pedir
como alza de salario los hijos de la pampa.
Así mandan de arriba, de la bolsa con dólares,
así recibe la orden el enano traidor,
así los generales hacen de policías,
así se pudre el tronco del árbol de la patria.

THEY RECEIVE INSTRUCTIONS
AGAINST CHILE

But we have to see behind all them, there is something
behind the traitors and the gnawing rats,
an empire which sets the table,
and serves up the nourishment and the bullets.
They want to repeat in you their great success in Greece.
Greek playboys at the banquet, and bullets
for the people in the mountains: we'll have to destroy the
    flight
of the new Victory of Samothrace, we'll have to hang,
kill, lose men, sink the murderous knife
held to us from New York, we'll have to use fire
to break the spirit of the man who was emerging
in all countries as if born
from the earth that had been splashed with blood.
We have to arm Chiang and the vicious Videla,
give them money for prisons, wings
so they can bomb their own populations, give them
a handout, a few dollars, and they do the rest,
they lie, bribe, dance on the dead bodies
and their first ladies wear the most expensive minks.
The suffering of the people does not matter: copper
executives need this sacrifice: facts are facts:
the generals retire from the army and serve
as vice-presidents of the Chuquicamata Copper Firm,
and in the nitrate works the "Chilean" general
decides with his trailing sword how much the natives
may mention when they ask for a raise in wages.
In this way they decide from above, from the roll of
    dollars,
in this way the dwarf traitor receives his instructions,
and the generals act as the police force,
and the trunk of the tree of the country rots.

                    Translated by Robert Bly
                    and James Wright

LOS ENIGMAS

Me habéis preguntado qué hila el crustaceo entre sus
    patas de oro
y os respondo: El mar lo sabe.
Me decís qué espera la ascidia en su campana trans-
    parente? Qué espera?
Yo os digo, espera como vosotros el tiempo.
Me preguntáis a quién alcanza el abrazo del alga
    Macrocustis?
Indagadlo, indagadlo a cierta hora, en cierto mar que
    conozco.
Sin duda me preguntaréis por el marfil maldito del
    narwhal, para que yo os conteste
de qué modo el unicornio marino agoniza arponeado.
Me preguntáis tal vez por las plumas alcionarias que
    tiemblan
en los puros orígenes de la marea austral?
Y sobre la construcción cristalina del pólipo habéis
    barajado, sin duda
una pregunta más, desgranándola ahora?
Queréis saber la eléctrica materia de las púas del fondo?
    La armada estalactita que camina quebrándose?
    El anzuelo del pez pescador, la música extendida
    en la profundidad como un hilo en el agua?

Yo os quiero decir que esto lo sabe el mar, que la vida
    en sus arcas
es ancha como la arena, innumerable y pura
y entre las uvas sanguinarias el tiempo ha pulido
la dureza de un pétalo, la luz de la medusa
y ha desgranado el ramo de sus hebras corales
desde una cornucopia de nácar infinito.

ENIGMAS

You've asked me what the lobster is weaving there with
    his golden feet?
I reply, the ocean knows this.
You say, what is the ascidia waiting for in its trans-
    parent bell? What is it waiting for?
I tell you it is waiting for time, like you.
You ask me whom the Macrocystis alga hugs in its arms?
Study, study it, at a certain hour, in a certain sea I know.
You question me about the wicked tusk of the narwhal,
    and I reply by describing
how the sea unicorn with the harpoon in it dies.
You enquire about the kingfisher's feathers,
which tremble in the pure springs of the southern tides?
Or you've found in the cards a new question touching on
    the crystal architecture
of the sea anemone, and you'll deal that to me now?
You want to understand the electric nature of the ocean
    spines?
  The armored stalactite that breaks as it walks?
  The hook of the angler fish, the music stretched out
in the deep places like a thread in the water?

I want to tell you the ocean knows this, that life in its
    jewel boxes
is endless as the sand, impossible to count, pure,
and among the blood-colored grapes time has made the
    petal
hard and shiny, made the jellyfish full of light
and untied its knot, letting its musical threads fall
from a horn of plenty made of infinite mother-of-
    pearl.

Yo no soy sino la red vacía que adelanta
ojos humanos, muertos en aquellas tinieblas,
dedos acostumbrados al triángulo, medidas
de un tímido hemisferio de naranja.

Anduve como vosotros escarbando
la estrella interminable,
y en mi red, en la noche, me desperté desnudo,
única presa, pez encerrado en el viento.

PART XIV, called "The Immense Ocean," is a great poem to the Pacific
Ocean, its islands and creatures. Many of the poems have a richness
like the *Residencia* poems. "Enigmas" is the seventeenth of the twenty-
four poems in this section.

I am nothing but the empty net which has gone on
    ahead
of human eyes, dead in those darknesses,
of fingers accustomed to the triangle, longitudes
on the timid globe of an orange.

I walked around as you do, investigating
the endless star,
and in my net, during the night, I woke up naked,
the only thing caught, a fish trapped inside the wind.

Translated by Robert Bly

COMPAÑEROS DE VIAJE

(1921)

Luego llegué a la capital, vagamente impregnado
de niebla y lluvia. Qué calles eran ésas?
Los trajes de 1921 pululaban
en un olor atroz de gas, café y ladrillos.
Entre los estudiantes pasé sin comprender,
reconcentrando en mí las paredes, buscando
cada tarde en mi pobre poesía las ramas,
las gotas y la luna que se habían perdido.
Acudí al fondo de ella, sumergiéndome
cada tarde en sus aguas, agarrando impalpables
estímulos, gaviotas de un mar abandonado,
hasta cerrar los ojos y naufragar en medio
de mi propia substancia.

                    Fueron tinieblas, fueron
sólo escondidas, húmedas hojas del subsuelo?
De qué materia herida se desgranó la muerte
hasta tocar mis miembros, conducir mi sonrisa
y cavar en las calles un pozo desdichado?

    Salí a vivir: crecí y endurecido
fuí por los callejones miserables,
sin compasión, cantando en las fronteras
del delirio. Los muros se llenaron de rostros:
ojos que no miraban la luz, aguas torcidas
que iluminaba un crimen, patrimonios
de solitario orgullo, cavidades
llenas de corazones arrasados.
Con ellos fuí: sólo en su coro

FRIENDS ON THE ROAD

(1921)

Then I arrived at the capital, vaguely saturated
with fog and rain. What streets were those?
The garments of 1921 were breeding
in an ugly smell of gas, coffee, and bricks.
I walked among the students without understanding,
pulling the walls inside me, searching
each day into my poor poetry for the branches,
the drops of rain, and the moon, that had been lost.
I went deep into it for help, sinking
each evening into its waters, grasping
energies I could not touch, the seagulls of a deserted sea,
until I closed my eyes and was shipwrecked in the middle
of my own body.
        Were these things dark shadows,
were they only hidden damp leaves stirred up from the
     soil?
What was the wounded substance from which death was
     pouring out
until it touched my arms and legs, controlled my smile,
and dug a well of pain in the streets?

I went out into life: I grew and was hardened,
I walked through the hideous back alleys
without compassion, singing out on the frontiers
of delirium. The walls filled with faces:
eyes that did not look at light, twisted waters
lit up by a crime, legacies
of solitary pride, holes
filled with hearts that had been condemned and torn
     down.
I walked with them: it was only in that chorus

mi voz reconoció las soledades
donde nació.

Entré a ser hombre
cantando entre las llamas, acogido
por compañeros de condición nocturna
que cantaron conmigo en los mesones,
y que me dieron más de una ternura,
más de una primavera defendida
por sus hostiles manos,
único fuego, planta verdadera
de los desmoronados arrabales.

PART XV, the final section, is called "I Am." It contains thirty-eight autobiographical poems, of which we have chosen the fourth, describing his school days in Santiago when he was seventeen. The first poem of the section touches on the frontier in the year he was born, and the last records the day, February 5, 1949, when *Canto General* was finished, "a few months before the forty-fifth year of my age."

that my voice refound the solitudes
where it was born.

I finally became a man
singing among the flames, accepted
by friends who find their place in the night,
who sang with me in the taverns,
and who gave me more than a single kindness,
something they had defended with their fighting hands,
which was more than a spring,
a fire unknown elsewhere, the natural foliage
of the places slowly falling down at the city's edge.

Translated by Robert Bly
and James Wright

from

Odas Elementales

1954–1957

ODA A LOS CALCETINES

Me trajo Maru Mori
un par
de calcetines
que tejió con sus manos
de pastora,
dos calcetines suaves
como liebres.
En ellos
metí los pies
como en
dos
estuches
tejidos
con hebras del
crepúsculo
y pellejo de ovejas.
Violentos calcetines,
mis pies fueron
dos pescados
de lana,
dos largos tiburones
de azul ultramarino
atravesados
por una trenza de oro,
dos gigantescos mirlos,
dos cañones:
mis pies
fueron honrados
de este modo
por
estos
celestiales

ODE TO MY SOCKS

Maru Mori brought me
a pair
of socks
which she knitted herself
with her sheepherder's hands,
two socks as soft
as rabbits.
I slipped my feet
into them
as though into
two
cases
knitted
with threads of
twilight
and goatskin.
Violent socks,
my feet were
two fish made
of wool,
two long sharks
sea-blue, shot
through
by one golden thread,
two immense blackbirds,
two cannons:
my feet
were honored
in this way
by
these
heavenly

calcetines.
Eran
tan hermosos
que por primera vez
mis pies me parecieron
inaceptables
come dos decrépitos
bomberos, bomberos,
indignos
de aquel fuego
bordado,
de aquellos luminosos
calcetines.

Sin embargo
resistí
la tentación aguda
de guardarlos
como los colegiales
preservan
las luciérnagas,
como los eruditos
coleccionan
documentos sagrados,
resistí
el impulso furioso
de ponerlos
en una jaula
de oro
y darles cada día
alpiste
y pulpa de melón rosado.
Como descubridores
que en la selva
entregan el rarísimo

socks.
They were
so handsome
for the first time
my feet seemed to me
unacceptable
like two decrepit
firemen, firemen
unworthy
of that woven
fire,
of those glowing
socks.

Nevertheless
I resisted
the sharp temptation
to save them somewhere
as schoolboys
keep
fireflies,
as learned men
collect
sacred texts,
I resisted
the mad impulse
to put them
into a golden
cage
and each day give them
birdseed
and pieces of pink melon.
Like explorers
in the jungle who hand
over the very rare

venado verde
al asador
y se lo comen
con remordimiento,
estiré
los pies
y me enfundé
los
bellos
calcetines
y
luego los zapatos.

Y es ésta
la moral de mi oda:
dos veces es belleza
la belleza
y lo que es bueno es doblemente
bueno
cuando se trata de dos calcetines
de lana
en el invierno.

green deer
to the spit
and eat it
with remorse,
I stretched out
my feet
and pulled on
the magnificent
socks
and then my shoes.

The moral
of my ode is this:
beauty is twice
beauty
and what is good is doubly
good
when it is a matter of two socks
made of wool
in winter.

Translated by Robert Bly

ODA A LA SANDÍA

El árbol del verano
intenso,
invulnerable,
es todo cielo azul,
sol amarillo,
cansancio a goterones,
es una espada
sobre los caminos,
un zapato quemado
en las ciudades:
la claridad, el mundo
nos agobian,
nos pegan
en los ojos
con polvareda,
con súbitos golpes de oro,
nos acosan
los pies
con espinitas,
con piedras calurosas,
y la boca
sufre
más que todos los dedos:
tienen sed
la garganta,
la dentadura,
los labios y la lengua:
queremos
beber las cataratas,
la noche azul,
el polo,
y entonces

ODE TO THE WATERMELON

The tree of intense
summer,
hard,
is all blue sky,
yellow sun,
fatigue in drops,
a sword
above the highways,
a scorched shoe
in the cities:
the brightness and the world
weigh us down,
hit us
in the eyes
with clouds of dust,
with sudden golden blows,
they torture
our feet
with tiny thorns,
with hot stones,
and the mouth
suffers
more than all the toes:
the throat
becomes thirsty,
the teeth,
the lips, the tongue:
we want to drink
waterfalls,
the dark blue night,
the South Pole,
and then

cruza el cielo
el más fresco de todos
los planetas,
la redonda, suprema
y celestial sandía.

Es la fruta del árbol de la sed.
Es la ballena verde del verano.

El universo seco
de pronto
tachonado
por este firmamento de frescura
deja caer
la fruta
rebosante:
se abren sus hemisferios
mostrando una bandera
verde, blanca, escarlata,
que se disuelve
en cascada, en azúcar,
en delicia!

Cofre del agua, plácida
reina
de la frutería,
bodega
de la profundidad, luna
terrestre!
Oh pura,
en tu abundancia
se deshacen rubíes
y uno
quisiera
morderte

the coolest of all
the planets crosses
the sky,
the round, magnificent,
star-filled watermelon.

It's a fruit from the thirst-tree.
It's the green whale of the summer.

The dry universe
all at once
given dark stars
by this firmament of coolness
lets the swelling
fruit
come down:
its hemispheres open
showing a flag
green, white, red,
that dissolves into
wild rivers, sugar,
delight!

Jewel box of water, phlegmatic
queen
of the fruitshops,
warehouse
of profundity, moon
on earth!
You are pure,
rubies fall apart
in your abundance,
and we
want
to bite into you,

hundiendo
en ti
la cara,
el pelo,
el alma!
Te divisamos
en la sed
como
mina o montaña
de espléndido alimento,
pero
te conviertes
entre la dentadura y el deseo
en sólo
fresca luz
que se deslíe
en manantial
que nos tocó
cantando.
Y así
no pesas
en la siesta
abrasadora,
no pesas,
sólo
pasas
y tu gran corazón de brasa fría
se convirtió en el agua
de una gota.

to bury our
face
in you, and
our hair, and
the soul!
When we're thirsty
we glimpse you
like
a mine or a mountain
of fantastic food,
but
among our longings and our teeth
you change
simply
into cool light
that slips in turn into
spring water
that touched us once
singing.
And that is why
you don't weigh us down
in the siesta hour
that's like an oven,
you don't weigh us down,
you just
go by
and your heart, some cold ember,
turned itself into a single
drop of water.

Translated by Robert Bly

ODA A LA SAL

Esta sal
del salero
yo la ví en los salares.
Sé que
no
van a creerme,
pero
canta,
canta la sal, la piel
de los salares,
canta
con una boca ahogada
por la tierra.
Me estremecí en aquellas
soledades
cuando escuché
la voz
de
la sal
en el desierto.
Cerca de Antofagasta
toda
la pampa salitrosa
suena:
es una
voz
quebrada,
un lastimero
canto.
Luego en sus cavidades
la sal gema, montaña
de una luz enterrada,

ODE TO SALT

I saw the salt
in this shaker
in the salt flats.
I know
you
will never believe me,
but
it sings,
the salt sings, the hide
of the salt plains,
it sings
through a mouth smothered
by earth.
I shuddered in those deep
solitudes
when I heard
the voice
of
the salt
in the desert.
Near Antofagasta
the entire
salt plain
speaks:
it is a
broken
voice,
a song full
of grief.
Then in its own mines
rock salt, a mountain
of buried light,

catedral transparente,
cristal del mar, olvido
de las olas.

Y luego en cada mesa
de este mundo,
sal,
tu substancia
ágil
espolvoreando
la luz vital
sobre
los alimentos.
Preservadora
de las antiguas
bodegas del navío,
descubridora
fuiste
en el océano,
materia
adelantada
en los desconocidos, entreabiertos
senderos de la espuma.
Polvo del mar, la lengua
de ti recibe un beso
de la noche marina:
el gusto funde en cada
sazonado manjar tu oceanía
y así la mínima,
la minúscula
ola del salero
nos enseña
no sólo su doméstica blancura,
sino el sabor central del infinito.

a cathedral through which light passes,
crystal of the sea, abandoned
by the waves.

And then on every table
on this earth,
salt,
your nimble
body
pouring out
the vigorous light
over
our foods.
Preserver
of the stores
of the ancient ships,
you were
an explorer
in the ocean,
substance
going first
over the unknown, barely open
routes of the sea-foam.
Dust of the sea, the tongue
receives a kiss
of the night sea from you:
taste recognizes
the ocean in each salted morsel,
and therefore the smallest,
the tiniest
wave of the shaker
brings home to us
not only your domestic whiteness
but the inward flavor of the infinite.

Translated by Robert Bly

THE LAMB AND THE PINECONE

(An interview with Pablo Neruda by Robert Bly)

A great river of images has flowed into your poetry, as well as into the poetry of Lorca, Aleixandre, Vallejo, and Hernández—an outpouring of poetry from the very roots of poetry. Why has the greatest poetry in the twentieth century appeared in the Spanish language?

I must tell you it is very nice to hear such a thing from an American poet. Of course we believe in enthusiasm too, but still we are all modest workers—we must not make too many comparisons. I must tell you two different things about poetry in Spanish. In the sixteenth and seventeenth centuries Spanish poetry was great—you had such giants as Góngora, Quevedo, Lope de Vega, and many, many others. Then, for three centuries after that, no poetry—a very, very small poetry. Finally, the generation of Lorca, Alberti, and Aleixandre wrote a large poetry again—they rose up against this small poetry. How, and why? We should remember that this generation of poets is coincident with the political awakening of Spain as a republic, the awakening of a great country that was asleep. Suddenly they had all the energy and strength of a man waking. I told about that in my poem, "How Spain Was," which I am sure you remember from our reading at the Poetry Center last night. Unfortunately, you see what happened. The Franco revolt. It sent into exile and to death so many of the poets. That happened with Miguel Hernández, Lorca, and Antonio Machado, who was really a classic of the century.

Poetry in South America is a different matter altogether. You see there are in our countries rivers which have no names, trees which nobody knows, and birds

156

which nobody has described. It is easier for us to be sur-realistic because everything we know is new. Our duty, then, as we understand it, is to express what is unheard of. Everything has been painted in Europe, everything has been sung in Europe. But not in America. In that sense, Whitman was a great teacher. Because what is Whitman? He was not only intensely conscious, but he was open-eyed! He had tremendous eyes to see every-thing—he taught us to see things. He was our poet.

Whitman has clearly had much more influence on the Spanish poets than on the North American poets. Why didn't the North American poets understand him? Was it because of the influence of England?

Perhaps, perhaps the intellectualist influence of Eng-land. Also many of the American poets just following Eliot thought that Whitman was too rustic, too primi-tive. But he is not so simple—Whitman—he's a compli-cated man and the best of him is when he is most compli-cated. He had eyes open to the world and he taught us about poetry and many other things. We have loved him very much. Eliot never had much influence with us. He's too intellectual perhaps, we are too primitive. And then everyone has to choose a road—a refined and intellectual way, or a more brotherly, general way, trying to em-brace the world around you, to discover the new world.

In his essays, Eliot directed attention toward tradition. But the suggestion you made seems to be that really South America has no tradition—America has no tradi-tion—and admitting this lack of tradition has opened up things.

That is an interesting thing. We do have to mention that in some South American poets you can see the trace of very old ways of thought and expression, Indian ways of thought in Vallejo, for instance. César Vallejo has something that comes from very deep in his country, Peru, which is an Indian country. He is a wonderful poet, as you know.

As for a literary tradition, what tradition could we have? The Spanish poetry of the 19th century was a very poor poetry—rhetorical and false—postromantic in the worst way. They never did have a good romantic poet. They had no Shelley, no Goethe. Nothing of the sort. No, no. Rhetorical and empty.

Your poetry presents a vision of affection between people, an affection between man and animals, compassion for plants and snakes, and a certain give and take between man and his unconscious. Most modern poets present a very different vision. How do you feel about that?

Well, I make a distinction between kinds of poetry. I am not a theoretician, but I do see as one kind of poetry the poetry which is written in closed rooms. I'll give as an example Mallarmé, a very great French poet. I have sometimes seen photographs of his room; they were full of little beautiful objects—"abanicos"—fans. He used to write beautiful poems on fans. But his rooms were stuffy, all full of curtains, no air. He is a great poet of closed rooms and it seems that many of the New World poets follow this tradition: they don't open the windows and you not only have to open the window but come through the windows and live with rivers and animals and beasts. I would say to young poets of my country and of Latin America—perhaps this is our tradition—to discover things, to be in the sea, to be in the mountains, and approach every living thing. And how can you not love such an approach to life, that has such extravagant surprises?

I live by a very rough sea in Isla Negra—my house is there—and I am never tired of being alone looking at the sea and working there. It is a perpetual discovery for me. I don't know, maybe I am a foolish 19th century nature lover like your great writer Thoreau, and other contemplative writers. I am not contemplative, but I think that is a great part of a poet's life.

You have fought many political battles, fighting seriously and steadily like a bear, and yet you have not ended up obsessed with political matters like Tolstoy, or embittered. Your poetry seems to become more and more human, and affectionate. Now how do you explain that?

You see, I come from a country which is very political. Those who fight have great support from the masses. Practically all the writers of Chile are out to the left—there are almost no exceptions. We feel supported and understood by our own people. That gives us great security and the numbers of people who support us are very great. You see the elections in Chile are won by one side or the other by few votes only. As poets we are really in touch with the people, which is very rare. I read my poems everywhere in my country—every village, every town—for years and years, and I feel it is my duty to do it. It is a tiresome thing, but partly from that has come my attachment to politics. I have seen so much the misery of my country. The poverty I see—I cannot get away from that.

Only in recent years have the people in the United States begun to realize what South American literature is. They still know very little about it.

I think the problem here is a matter of translation. We need to have more North American writers translated into Spanish and South American poetry and literature translated into English. The delegation of the P.E.N. Club of Chile have shown me a list of books they have drawn up. The list contains one hundred basic works in South American literature which could be read by all the North American people. They intend to look for support for this project and plan to present it as a motion during the P.E.N. Congress. That is a good idea. I don't know if the P.E.N. Club can support it, but someone should support the project. The whole problem of translation is a great and serious one. Imagine—that Vallejo's work has never been published in the United States! Only the twenty poems published by your Sixties Press.

I know you have come to believe that among the many enemies mankind has are gods. I think you said you first felt this in Rangoon. But don't the gods come from the unconscious of men, just as poems do? In what sense then are they enemies?

In the beginning gods help like poems. Man makes gods who help men. But afterward men overpower gods and then bankruptcy.

I have a good question for you. Do you think you have ever lived before?

I don't know . . . I don't think—I will try to inquire!

Tolstoy said a new consciousness was developing in humanity, like a new organ, and that the governments had set themselves to stop the growth of this new consciousness. Do you think this is true?

In general, you see, governments have never understood anywhere in the world the spirit of writers and poets. That is the general thing which we are going to cure. How? Producing and writing. You poets are doing a wonderful thing in the United States which I have seen from your lectures in public and all that. You are awakening a new thing since you are defending this spirit you are talking about.

César Vallejo, after struggling through or plunging into a long period of surrealism (The Trilce Poems), *came out into a very human simplicity in* Poemas Humanos. *You also passed through a long period of surrealist poetry in* Residencia en la Tierra *and then came out into the simplicity of* Odas Elementales. *Isn't it strange you have both followed the same path?*

I love Vallejo. I always admired him, we were brothers. Nevertheless, we were very different. Race especially. He was Peruvian. He was a very Peruvian man and to me Peruvian man is something interesting. We came from different worlds. I have never thought about what you tell me. I like very much the way you approach us— that you bring us near each other in our work worlds. I never thought of it. I like it.

What was Vallejo like when you were in a room with him? Was he excitable, or calm and broody?

Vallejo was usually very serious, very solemn, you see, with great dignity. He had a very high forehead and he was small in stature, and he kept himself very much aloof. But among friends—I don't know if he was this way with others but he was with us—I have seen him jumping with happiness, jumping. So I knew at least these two sides of him.

161

People often talk of the "Indian element" which they see in much Latin American poetry and fiction. What is this "Indian element" exactly?

In Vallejo it shows itself as a subtle way of thought, a way of expression that is not direct, but oblique. I don't have it. I am a Castilian poet. In Chile we defend the Indians and almost all South Americans have some Indian blood, I do too. But I don't think my work is in any way Indian.

In Residencia *your poems dug deeper and deeper into despair, like a man digging into black earth. Then you turned away in another direction, and your poetry moved more and more toward a simplicity. Did this come about partly because the Spanish Civil War made it absolutely clear how much the people needed help?*

You say that very well—it is true. You see, when I wrote *Residencia One and Two* I was living in India. I was twenty-one, twenty-two, and twenty-three years old. I was isolated from the Indian people, whom I didn't know, and also from the English people whom I didn't understand, nor did they understand me, and I was in a very lonely situation. I was in an exciting country which I couldn't penetrate, which I couldn't understand well. They were lonely days and years for me. In 1934 I was transferred as consul to Madrid. The Civil War did help me and inspire me to live more near the people, to understand more and to be more natural. For the first time I felt that I belonged to a community.

Have your opinions of Rilke and the "Poetas Celestes" (Divine Poets) changed at all since the poem you wrote attacking them?

162

Yes, I must say I have been mistaken many times in my life. I was dogmatic and foolish. But the trend of my ideas is as it was. Only in my exaggeration I was mistaken, because he is a great poet, just as Kafka is a great writer. Excuse me, but the contradictions—one sees them only when life rolls on, one sees one has been mistaken.

Many people feel that the quality of literary work being done now shows a decline from the work being done thirty years ago? Do you think so?

No, no. I think the creativity is strong. I see so many new forms in poetry now in the young poets I have never seen before. There is no more fear of experience. Before there was a great fear of breaking the mold and now there is no more of this fear. It is wonderful.

How come you don't have that fear of experience?

It took me a lot of time to have no fear. When I was a young poet I was full of fear like a real rat in a corner. When I was a very young poet I was afraid to break all the laws which were enforced on us by the critics. But now there is no more of this. All the young poets come in and say what they like and do what they like.

In one of your essays you described something that happened to you as a boy which you thought has had a great influence on your poetry. There was a fence in your backyard. Through a hole in it one day a small hand passed through to you a gift—a toy lamb. And you went into the house and came back and handed back through the hole the thing you loved most—a pinecone.

Yes, that boy passed me a lamb, a woolen lamb. It was beautiful.

You said that somehow this helped you to understand that if you give something to humanity you'll get something else back even more beautiful.

Your memory is wonderful, and this is exactly right. I learned much from that in my childhood. This exchange of gifts—mysterious—settled deep inside me like a sedimentary deposit.

The interview took place
June 12, 1966, in New York.

Selected Poems of
CÉSAR VALLEJO

WHAT IF AFTER SO MANY WINGS
OF BIRDS

César Vallejo is not a poet of the partially authentic feeling, as most poets in the English tradition are, but a poet of the absolutely authentic. He does not hide part of his life, and describe only the more "poetic" parts. He lived a difficult life, full of fight, and in describing it never panders to a love of pleasantries nor a love of vulgarity. He had a tremendous feeling for, and love of, his family—his father, his mother, and his brothers—which he expresses with simple images of great resonance. There is a tenderness, as in Chaucer. His wildness and savagery exist side by side with it. The wildness and savagery rest on a clear compassion for others, and a clear intuition into his own inward directions. He sees roads inside himself. In the remarkable intensity with which he follows a thought or an image, there is a kind of heroism. Like a great fish, he follows the poem wherever it goes in the sea.

II

César Vallejo was born March 15, 1892, in a small mining town in Northern Peru. His family had Indian blood on both sides. The poem called "To My Brother Miguel" describes the mood of the house—a Catholic house, with devotions and prayers. About the family, James Wright has written:

His home town was small and provincial, with an ancient and living tradition of large, affectionate families who were of necessity mobilized, as it were, against the physical and spiritual onslaughts of death in its ancient and modern forms: disease, undernourishment, and cold on the one hand; the offi-

169

cials of the tungsten mines on the other . . . he is always returning to poems about his family, poems which in their intensity and daring are more beautiful than any other poems on the subject that I have seen.

He went off at eighteen to the university in Trujillo. After studying and working on and off for several years, he graduated there when he was twenty-three. He was already at work on a book. He supported himself after graduation teaching in primary schools. He worked on his book another three years, and it was published in Lima in 1919. He called it *Los Heraldos Negros*, suggesting horsemen, maybe riding black horses, who come with messages, messages from death. It is a staggering book, sensual, prophetic, affectionate, wild. It has a kind of compassion for God, and compassion for death, who has so many problems, and it moves with incredible leaps of imagination. I think it is the greatest single collection of poems I have ever read.

The next year he went home for a visit, and got involved, without intending to, in a provincial political feud. His politics were known, and his imprisonment may have been revenge for those. His sentence was three months in a jail in Trujillo. There he wrote some of the poems for his second book, *Trilce*. *Trilce* is difficult, even for people who read poetry a great deal. The poems are like flashes of light in a room already light. The associative thinking in them takes place with incredible speed, and most are oblique, surrealist, interior, like willows, "almost air." Their surrealist airiness is at the opposite pole from Neruda's dense *Residencia* poems, which are borne down by his entangled, intestinal, jungle surrealism. The *Trilce* poems are so difficult that very few of them have been translated into English.

The year after it was published, Vallejo lost his teaching job in Lima, and decided to go to Paris as a stringer for a Trujillo newspaper. After all, the surrealists lived in Paris. Once there he was poor right away, and despite occasional translating and newspaper jobs, his poverty returned on and off for the rest of his life. There were many South American intellectuals in Paris, and in any case the French tended to regard all South Americans as second class citizens. The poverty he experienced was not a playful bohemian poverty, but something permanent, a state that he could not get out of. He felt close to others at the bottom of the ladder, and he has a number of compassionate poems written to and for French whores that he knew. His "Poem To Be Read and Sung" appears to be one of them. He remained in Europe for fifteen years and never returned to America. Somewhere I read that he developed elaborate theories on how you could step off a subway car without wearing out the soles of your shoes; how to cross your legs so as not to wear out your trouser knees. He read much French poetry, and met Artaud and others. When the Depression came, he thought as much about the problem of poverty as about the problem of poetry, and evidently more about other people's poverty than his own. He took the Communist movement seriously, and was a committed Marxist. In 1928 he went on a visit to Russia, and the next year interviewed Mayakovsky in Moscow. In 1930 the French deported him and his French wife, Georgette.

They went to Spain, and so Vallejo experienced Spain in the early Thirties, when Lorca and his generation were writing their fantastically rich surrealist poems. In Spain Vallejo wrote a novel, a book of essays, and two plays. None of his reporting or essays or plays from this period have been translated.

In 1932 he returned to Paris, and except for short

visits to Spain, lived in Paris with Georgette until his death six years later. Franco's invasion of the Spanish Republic in 1936 affected his life profoundly. During these years Vallejo worked constantly for the Republic, gathering money and support, writing. A small book of his poems about the Civil War, called *España, aparte de mí esta Cáliz* (Spain, Take This Cup from Me), written' shortly before he died, was printed in Spain, as Miguel Hernández' poems were, by the Republican soldiers themselves.

His third large collection of poems, following *Los Heraldos Negros* and *Trilce*, is the volume called *Poemas Humanos*. It is not clear when the poems making up *Poemas Humanos* were written. During his last year, he spent some months preparing the collection for publication; he rewrote many, and possibly wrote a number of new ones. If a poem we have translated here has a date following it, the date is that of the final draft of the poem, and was marked on the manuscript by Vallejo himself sometime in September, October, November, or December 1937. Whether the undated ones were written at that time, or years before, and if written years before, were considered unsalvageable, or already finished, no one seems to know. At the start of the *Poemas Humanos* group I have put some prose poems which apparently belong to an unfinished book called *Codigo Civil*, but which are always published with *Poemas Humanos* poems, though written during his earliest years in Paris.

He exhausted himself in the winter of 1937–38, working for the refugees, writing poems, anguishing over the beating the Left was taking in the Civil War, the deaths in Spain, the defeat of so much work by so many men. In the spring of 1938 Vallejo developed a fever the European doctors could not diagnose or treat, and he died in Paris on April 15, 1938, while it was raining. He was

a Pisces, and had predicted years earlier: "I will die in
Paris on a rainy day." His body was buried in Mont-
rouge Cemetery; several French writers and artists were
at the graveside. His wife Georgette, who had helped him
stay alive for years, later moved to Lima, where she still
lives.

III

I notice that contemporary English poets and critics
want English poetry to be tied in to "history," by which
they mean linguistic history, the various layers of mean-
ing a given word has taken on, the encrustations an
iambic line has taken on by floating face down through
the centuries, the curious angles an idea has chipped into
it by being misunderstood by dopes in the Elizabethan,
in the Tudor. . . . The outcome of this longing is that
the word is never fresh, the line has fused vertebrae, and
the poem does not convey *thinking*, but instead contains
portraits of ideas, like those "Wanted" posters issued
by police departments.

But Vallejo's art shows us what it's like not to go
about recapturing ideas, but actually to think. We feel
the flow of thought, its power like an underground river
finding its way for the first time through some shifted
ground—even he doesn't know where it will come out.

César Vallejo embodies the history of mankind, as
Jung and Freud do, not by sprinkling the dust of the
past on his words, but by thinking his way backward and
forward through it.

He loves thinkers and refers to them again and again
in his poems—Marx, Feuerbach, Freud, Socrates,
Aristotle—at the same time he respects human suffering
so much he is afraid that his thought and theirs might be
too private:

173

A cripple walks by giving his arm to a child.
After that I'm supposed to read André Breton?

In *Poemas Humanos* especially, Vallejo suggests so well
the incredible weight of daily life, how it pulls men down;
carrying a day is like carrying a mountain. And what
the weight of daily life wants to pull us down to is medi-
ocrity. He hates it. I notice that women respond imme-
diately to this horror of mediocrity in Vallejo, a horror
women share, being often pushed by circumstances into
monotonous, "one-stringed" living, without a trace of
wildness. Vallejo wants life and literature to be intense
or not at all.

> And what if after so many wings of birds,
> the stopped bird doesn't survive!
> It would be better then, really,
> if it were all swallowed up, and let's end it!

*   *   *

It is this marvelous intensity that is his mark for me.
Many poets we all know are able to associate with con-
siderable speed when there are not many mammal emo-
tions around—Wallace Stevens, for example, creates a
philosophical calm in his poetry, inside of which he asso-
ciates quite rapidly—but when anger or anguish enter
the poem, they become tongue-tied, or lapse into clichés.
Vallejo does just the opposite. Under the pressure of
powerful human feeling, of anger, or self-doubt, or com-
passion, he leaps about wildly, each leap throwing him
farther out into the edges of consciousness, and at the
same time deeper into the "depths." As he says, "Don't
we rise to go down?"

Robert Bly

174

THOUGHTS ON CÉSAR VALLEJO

When I first translated a poem by César Vallejo, one summer night, I knew that I was in the presence of a personality as appealing as any I had met before. The man is a mystic who is skeptical, a fugitive deeply in love with his home, an isolated man who cannot put aside his painful communion with others. He expresses in masculine tones the massed, present anger of the poor man. And more, there is something very ancient in this Vallejo which gives his voice a force a reader seldom confronts. It is the authority of the oral poets of the Andes, those fashioners of the "harawi," a mystical, inward-turning complaint. Its tones can still be heard in lyrics sung in the mountains of Peru and played on records in the homesick barrios of Lima. Born in the Andes of an Indian mother, César Vallejo took this folk form in its essentials, discarding what was superficial and picturesque, and made it the echo chamber for a modern and surrealistic speech.

The art of Vallejo is a way of making disparate things live with each other: a young girl nurses the hour, a man points with a God-murdering finger, a man drowns the length of a throat, a stone walks crouched over in the soul. His ability to astonish with metaphor is matched by a talent for shifting from idiom to idiom. In poems like "Agape," the idiom has a primal simplicity. In, for instance, "The Weary Circles," the poem rises to piercing surrealistic metaphors, and then suddenly drops into the tough, blunt colloquial. Through his work the line springs from or opens into common images of simple and singular life: bread, the act of eating, of putting on your clothes, the pains in the bones, the weather of the day. His most grave poetry is seeded with the tags and catchwords of common speech, those small phrases which all men use to guard their helplessness before the incomprehensible. Other American poets have his ability to create startling metaphors, but no one that I know of has managed to express with such precision and such range the impossible relationship of a man to his own terrible self and his own terrrible times. He whimpers, he denounces, he poses, he sees through himself, he ruminates; he does all the unimaginable things that everyone does. Compared with Vallejo, other poets seem afraid of the sound of their own voices.

He is at once the most immediate and the most isolated of poets, this man who is always talking to someone who cannot answer. He is certainly a poet of stature, and has been recognized for a long time as one of the greatest of the Latin Americans. Now his light begins to fall the length of the hemisphere.

John Knoepfle

from

The Black Riders

(Los Heraldos Negros)

1918

LOS HERALDOS NEGROS

Hay golpes en la vida, tan fuertes . . . Yo no sé!
Golpes como del odio de Dios; como si ante ellos,
la resaca de todo lo sufrido
se empozara en el alma . . . Yo no sé!

Son pocos, pero son . . . Abren zanjas oscuras
en el rostro más fiero y en el lomo más fuerte.
Serán tal vez los potros de bárbaros atilas;
o los heraldos negros que nos manda la Muerte.

Son las caídas hondas de los Cristos del alma,
de alguna fe adorable que el Destino blasfema.
Esos golpes sangrientos son las crepitaciones
de algún pan que en la puerta del horno se nos quema.

Y el hombre . . . Pobre . . . pobre! Vuelve los ojos,
    como
cuando por sobre el hombro nos llama una palmada;
vuelve los ojos locos, y todo lo vivido
se empoza, como un charco de culpa, en la mirada.

Hay golpes en la vida, tan fuertes . . . Yo no sé!

THE BLACK RIDERS

There are blows in life so violent—I can't answer!
Blows as if from the hatred of God; as if before them,
the deep waters of everything lived through
were backed up in the soul . . . I can't answer!

Not many; but they exist . . . They open dark ravines
in the most ferocious face and in the most bull-like back.
Perhaps they are the horses of that heathen Attila,
or the black riders sent to us by Death.

They are the slips backward made by the Christs of the
    soul,
away from some holy faith that is sneered at by Events.
These blows that are bloody are the crackling sounds
from some bread that burns at the oven door.

And man . . . poor man! . . . poor man! He swings
    his eyes, as
when a man behind us calls us by clapping his hands;
swings his crazy eyes, and everything alive
is backed up, like a pool of guilt, in that glance.

There are blows in life so violent . . . I can't answer!

Translated by Robert Bly

LA ARAÑA

Es una araña enorme que ya no anda;
una araña incolora, cuyo cuerpo,
una cabeza y un abdomen, sangra.

Hoy la he visto de cerca. Y con qué esfuerzo
hacia todos los flancos
sus pies innumerables alargaba.
Y he pensado en sus ojos invisibles,
los pilotos fatales de la araña.

Es una araña que temblaba fija
en un filo de piedra;
el abdomen a un lado,
y al otro la cabeza.

Con tantos pies la pobre, y aún no puede
resolverse. Y, al verla
atónita en tal trance,
hoy me ha dado qué pena esa viajera.

Es una araña enorme, a quien impide
el abdomen seguir a la cabeza.
Y he pensado en sus ojos
y en sus pies numerosos . . .
¡Y me ha dado qué pena esa viajera!

THE SPIDER

It is a huge spider, which can no longer move;
a spider which is colorless, whose body,
a head and an abdomen, is bleeding.

Today I watched it with great care. With what tremen-
    dous energy
to every side
it was stretching out its many feet.
And I have been thinking of its invisible eyes,
the death-bringing pilots of the spider.

It is a spider which was shivering, fixed
on the sharp ridge of a stone;
the abdomen on one side,
and on the other, the head.

With so many feet the poor thing, and still it cannot
solve it! And seeing it
confused in such great danger,
what a strange pain that traveler has given me today!

It is a huge spider, whose abdomen
prevents him from following his head.
And I have been thinking of his eyes
and of his many, many feet . . .
And what a strange pain that traveler has given me!

Translated by Robert Bly

ROMERÍA

Pasamos juntos. El sueño
lame nuestros pies qué dulce;
y todo se desplaza en pálidas
renunciaciones sin dulce.

Pasamos juntos. Las muertas
almas, las que, cual nosotros,
cruzaron por el amor,
con enfermos pasos ópalos,
salen en sus lutos rígidos
y se ondulan en nosotros.

Amada, vamos al borde
frágil de un montón de tierra.
Va en aceite ungida el ala,
y en pureza. Pero un golpe,
al caer yo no sé dónde,
afila de cada lágrima
un diente hostil.

Y un soldado, un gran soldado,
heridas por charreteras,
se anima en la tarde heroica,
y a sus pies muestra entre risas,
como una gualdrapa horrenda,
el cerebro de la Vida.

Pasamos juntos, muy juntos,
invicta Luz, paso enfermo;
pasamos juntos las lilas
mostazas de un cementerio.

PILGRIMAGE

We go along together. The dream
laps so pleasantly at our feet;
and everything is distorted in pale
unpleasant renunciations.

We go along together. The dead
souls, who, like ourselves, crossed over
for the sake of love,
with halting opal footsteps
come out in their rigid mourning dresses
and undulate toward us.

Beloved, we walk on the fragile edge
of a heap of earth.
A wing goes by, anointed with oil,
with purity. But a blow,
falling somewhere I don't know of,
grinds a hostile tooth
out of every tear.

And a soldier, a huge soldier,
with wounds for epaulets,
gets bold in the heroic evening,
and laughing, he shows at his feet,
like a hideous pile of rags,
the brain of Life.

We go along together, close together,
halting footsteps, undefeated light;
we walk past the mustard lilacs
of a cemetery.

Translated by James Wright

BABEL

Dulce hogar sin estilo, fabricado
de un solo golpe y de una sola pieza
de cera tornasol. Y en el hogar
ella daña y arregla; a veces dice:
"El hospicio es bonito; aquí no más!"
¡Y otras veces se pone a llorar!

BABBLE

Meek house with no style, framed
with a single knock and a single piece
of rainbow wax. And in the house
she destroys and she cleans; says at times:
"The asylum is nice. Where? Here!"
Other times she breaks down and cries.

Translated by John Knoepfle

DESHOJACIÓN SAGRADA

Luna! Corona de un testa inmensa,
que te vas deshojando en sombras gualdas!
Roja corona de un Jesús que piensa
trágicamente dulce de esmeraldas!

Luna! Alocado corazón celeste
por qué bogas así, dentro la copa
llena de vino azul, hacia el oeste,
cual derrotada y dolorida popa?

Luna! Y a fuerza de volar en vano,
te holocaustas en ópalos dispersos:
tú eres tal vez mi corazón gitano
que vaga en el azul llorando versos! . . .

A DIVINE FALLING OF LEAVES

Moon: royal crown of an enormous head,
dropping leaves into yellow shadows as you go.
Red crown of a Jesus who broods
tragically, softly over emeralds!

Moon: reckless heart in heaven,
why do you row toward the west
in that cup filled with blue wine,
whose hull is defeated and sad?

Moon: it is no use flying away,
so you go up in a flame of scattered opals:
maybe you are my heart, who is like a gypsy,
who loafs in the sky, shedding poems like tears! . . .

Translated by James Wright

LA COPA NEGRA

La noche es una copa de mal. Un silbo agudo
del guardia la atraviesa, cual vibrante alfiler.
Oye, tú, mujerzuela, ¿cómo, si ya te fuiste,
la onda aún es negra y me hace aún arder?

La Tierra tiene bordes de féretro en la sombra.
Oye tú, mujerzuela, no vayas a volver.

Mi carne nada, nada
en la copa de sombra que me hace aún doler;
mi carne nada en ella,
como en un pantanoso corazón de mujer.

Ascua astral . . . He sentido
secos roces de arcilla
sobre mi loto diáfano caer.
Ah, mujer! Por ti existe
la carne hecha de instinto. A mujer!

Por eso ¡oh, negro cáliz! aun cuando ya te fuiste,
me ahogo con el polvo;
y piafan en mis carnes más ganas de beber!

THE BLACK CUP

The night is a cup of evil. A police whistle
cuts across it, like a vibrating pin.
Trampy woman, listen, how is it, if you have gone away,
that the wave is still black and still makes me flare up?

The Earth holds the edges of a coffin in its darkness.
Listen, tramp, you will never come back.

My flesh swims, swims
in that cup of darkness that still makes me grieve;
my flesh swims in there
as in the swampy heart of a woman.

Starlike coal . . . I have felt
dry rubbings of clay fall
over my transparent lotus.
Ah, woman! This flesh that is all
instinct exists for you. Ah, woman!

Because of this, black chalice! now that you are gone,
I smother in the dust,
and other desires to drink start pawing inside my flesh.

Translated by James Wright
and Robert Bly

HECES

Esta tarde llueve como nunca; y no
tengo ganas de vivir, corazón.

Esta tarde es dulce. Por qué no ha de ser?
Viste gracia y pena; viste de mujer.

Esta tarde en Lima llueve. Y yo recuerdo
las cavernas crueles de mi ingratitud;
mi bloque de hielo sobre su amapola,
más fuerte que su "No seas así!"

Mis violentas flores negras; y la bárbara
y enorme pedrada; y el trecho glacial.
Y pondrá el silencio de su dignidad
con óleos quemantes el punto final.

Por eso esta tarde, como nunca, voy
con este buho, con este corazón.

Y otras pasan; y viéndome tan triste,
toman un poquito de ti
en la abrupta arruga de mi hondo dolor.

Esta tarde llueve, llueve mucho. Y no
tengo ganas de vivir, corazón!

DOWN TO THE DREGS

This afternoon it rains as never before; and I
don't feel like staying alive, heart.

The afternoon is pleasant. Why shouldn't it be?
It is wearing grace and pain; it is dressed like a woman.

This afternoon in Lima it is raining. And I remember
the cruel caverns of my ingratitude;
my block of ice laid on her poppy,
stronger than her crying "Don't be this way!"

My violent black flowers; and the barbarous
and staggering blow with a stone; and the glacial pause.
And the silence of her dignity will pour
scalding oils on the end of the sentence.

Therefore, this afternoon, as never before, I walk
with this owl, with this heart.

And other women go past; and seeing me sullen,
they sip a little of you
in the abrupt furrow of my deep grief.

This afternoon it rains, rains endlessly. And I
don't feel like staying alive, heart.

Translated by James Wright

MEDIALUZ

He soñado una fuga. Y he soñado
tus encajes dispersos en la alcoba.
A lo largo de un muelle, alguna madre;
y sus quince años dando el seno a una hora.

He soñado una fuga. Un "para siempre"
suspirado en la escala de una proa;
he soñado una madre;
unas frescas matitas de verdura,
y el ajuar constelado de una aurora.

A lo largo de un muelle . . .
Y a lo largo de un cuello que se ahoga!

TWILIGHT

I have dreamed of flight. And I have dreamed
of your laces strewn in the bedroom.
I have dreamed of some mother walking the length of a
    wharf
and at fifteen nursing the hour.

I have dreamed of flight. A "forever"
sighed at a fo'c'sle ladder.
I have dreamed of a mother,
of fresh sprigs of table-greens,
and the stars stitched in bridals of the dawn.

       The length of a wharf . . .
the length of a drowning throat!

Translated by John Knoepfle

ÁGAPE

Hoy no ha venido nadie a preguntar;
ni me han pedido en esta tarde nada.

No he visto ni una flor de cementerio
en tan alegre procesión de luces.
Perdóname, Señor: qué poco he muerto!

En esta tarde todos, todos pasan
sin preguntarme ni pedirme nada.

Y no sé qué se olvidan y se queda
mal en mis manos, como cosa ajena.

He salido a la puerta,
y me da ganas de gritar a todos:
Si echan de menos algo, aquí se queda!

Porque en todas las tardes de esta vida,
yo no sé con qué puertas dan a un rostro,
y algo ajeno se toma el alma mía.

Hoy no ha venido nadie;
y hoy he muerto qué poco en esta tarde!

AGAPE

Today no one has come to inquire,
nor have they wanted anything from me this afternoon.

I have not seen a single cemetery flower
in so happy a procession of lights.
Forgive me, Lord! I have died so little!

This afternoon everyone, everyone goes by
without asking or begging me anything.

And I do not know what it is they forget, and it is
heavy in my hands like something stolen.

I have come to the door,
and I want to shout at everyone:
—If you miss something, here it is!

Because in all the afternoons of this life,
I do not know how many doors are slammed on a face,
and my soul takes something that belongs to another.

Today nobody has come;
and today I have died so little in the afternoon!

Translated by John Knoepfle

ROSA BLANCA

Me siento bien. Ahora
brilla un estoico hielo
en mí.
Me da risa esta soga
rubí
que rechina en mi cuerpo.

Soga sin fin,
como una
voluta
descendente
de
mal . . .
soga sanguínea y zurda
formada de
mil dagas en puntal.

Que vaya así, trenzando
sus rollos de crespón;
y que ate el gato trémulo
del Miedo al nido helado,
al último fogón.

Yo ahora estoy sereno,
con luz.
Y maya en mi Pacífico
un náufrago ataúd.

WHITE ROSE

I feel all right. Now
a stoical frost shines
in me.
It makes me laugh, this ruby-colored
rope
that creaks in my body.

Endless rope,
like a spiral
descending
from
evil . . .
rope, bloody and clumsy,
shaped by
a thousand waiting daggers.

Because it goes in this way, braiding
its rolls of funeral crepe,
and because it ties the quivering cat
of Fear to the frozen nest,
to the final fire.

Now surrounded by light
I am calm.
And out on my Pacific
a shipwrecked coffin mews.

Translated by James Wright

EL PAN NUESTRO

(para Alejandro Gamboa)

Se bebe el desayuno . . . Húmeda tierra
de cimenterio huele a sangre amada.
Ciudad de invierno . . . La mordaz cruzada
de una carreta que arrastrar parece
un emoción de ayuno encadenada!

Se quisiera tocar todas las puertas,
y preguntar por no sé quién; y luego
ver a los pobres, y, llorando quedos,
dar pedacitos de pan fresco a todos.
Y saquear a los ricos sus viñedos
con las dos manos santas
que a un golpe de luz
volaron desclavadas de la Cruz!

Pestaña matinal, no os levantéis!
¡El pan nuestro de cada día dánoslo,
Señor . . . !

Todos mis huesos son ajenos;
yo tal vez los robé!
Yo vine a darme lo que acaso estuvo
asignado para otro;
y pienso que, si no hubiera nacido,
otro pobre tomara este café!
Yo soy un mal ladrón . . . A dónde iré!

OUR DAILY BREAD

(for Alejandro Gamboa)

Breakfast is drunk down . . . Damp earth
of the cemetery gives off the fragrance of the precious
    blood.
City of winter . . . the mordant crusade
of a cart that seems to pull behind it
an emotion of fasting that cannot get free!

I wish I could beat on all the doors,
and ask for somebody; and then
look at the poor, and, while they wept softly,
give bits of fresh bread to them.
And plunder the rich of their vineyards
with those two blessed hands
which blasted the nails with one blow of light,
and flew away from the Cross!

Eyelash of morning, you cannot lift yourselves!
Give us our daily bread,
Lord . . . !

Every bone in me belongs to others;
and maybe I robbed them.
I came to take something for myself that maybe
was meant for some other man;
and I start thinking that, if I had not been born,
another poor man could have drunk this coffee.
I feel like a dirty thief . . . Where will I end?

Y en esta hora fría, en que la tierra
trasciende a polvo humano y es tan triste,
quisiera yo tocar todas las puertas,
y suplicar a no sé quién, perdón
y hacerle pedacitos de pan fresco
aquí, en el horno de mi corazón . . . !

And in this frigid hour, when the earth
has the odor of human dust and is so sad,
I wish I could beat on all the doors
and beg pardon from someone,
and make bits of fresh bread for him
here, in the oven of my heart . . . !

Translated by James Wright

PAGANA

Ir muriendo y cantando. Y bautizar la sombra
con sangre babilónica de noble gladiador.
Y rubricar los cuneiformes de la áurea alfombra
con la pluma del ruiseñor y la tinta azul del dolor.

La vida? Hembra proteica. Contemplarla asustada
escaparse en sus velos, infiel, falsa Judith;
verla desde la herida, y asirla en la mirada,
incrustando un capricho de cera en un rubí.

Mosto de Babilonia, Holofernes sin tropas,
en el árbol, cristiano yo colgué mi nidal;
la viña redentora negó amor a mis copas;
Judith, la vida aleve, sesgó su cuerpo hostial.

Tal un festín pagano. Y amarla hasta en la muerte,
mientras las venas siembran rojas perlas de mal;
y así volverse al polvo, conquistador sin suerte,
dejando miles de ojos de sangre en el puñal.

PAGAN WOMAN

To go along dying and singing. And to baptize the
    darkness
with Babylonian blood of a high-minded gladiator.
And to sign the cuneiforms of the gold carpet
with the nightingale's feather and the blue ink of pain.

Life? Woman of all shapes. To watch her, terrified,
escaping from her veils—false, treacherous Judith;
to see her from the wound, and seize her in a look,
imprinting a whim of wax right into the ruby.

Wine dregs of Babylonia, Holofernes without soldiers,
I have built my nest in the tree of Christ;
The savior vine would not give my chalices its love;
Judith, the faithless life, twisted her votive body.

What a pagan celebration! And to love her even to death,
while the veins sow red pearls of evil;
and so to return to dust, a conqueror with no luck,
leaving thousands of eyes of blood on the knife point.

Translated by Robert Bly

LOS DADOS ETERNOS

Para Manuel Gonzáles Prada, esta emoción bravía
y selecta, una de las que, con más entusiasmo, me ha
aplaudido el gran maestro.

Dios mío, estoy llorando el ser que vivo;
me pesa haber tomádote tu pan;
pero este pobre barro pensativo
no es costra fermentada en tu costado:
tú no tienes Marías que se van!

Dios mío, si tú hubieras sido hombre,
hoy supieras ser Dios;
pero tú, que estuviste siempre bien,
no sientes nada de tu creación.
Y el hombre sí te sufre: el Dios es él!

Hoy que en mis ojos brujos hay candelas,
como en un condenado,
Dios mío, prenderás todas tus velas,
y jugaremos con el viejo dado . . .
Tal vez ¡oh jugador! al dar la suerte
del universo todo,
surgirán las ojeras de la Muerte,
como dos ases fúnebres de lodo.

Dios mío, y esta noche sorda oscura,
ya no podrás jugar, porque la Tierra
es un dado roído y ya redondo
a fuerza de rodar a la aventura,
que no puede parar si no en un hueco,
en el hueco de inmensa sepultura.

THE ETERNAL DICE

*For Manuel González Prada, this wild and unique
feeling—one of those emotions which the great
master has admired most in my work.*

God of mine, I am weeping for the life that I live;
I am sorry to have stolen your bread;
but this wretched, thinking piece of clay
is not a crust formed in your side:
you have no Marys that abandon you!

My God, if you had been man,
today you would know how to be God,
but you always lived so well,
that now you feel nothing of your own creation.
And the man who suffers you: he is God!

Today, when there are candles in my witchlike eyes,
as in the eyes of a condemned man,
God of mine, you will light all your lamps,
and we will play with the old dice . . .
Gambler, when the whole universe, perhaps,
is thrown down,
the circled eyes of Death will turn up,
like two final aces of clay.

My God, in this muffled, dark night,
you can't play anymore, because the Earth
is already a die nicked and rounded
from rolling by chance;
and it can stop only in a hollow place,
in the hollow of the enormous grave.

Translated by James Wright

205

LOS ANILLOS FATIGADOS

Hay ganas de volver, de amar, de no ausentarse
y hay ganas de morir, combatido por dos
aguas encontradas que jamás han de istmarse.

Hay ganas de un gran beso que amortaje a la Vida,
que acaba en el África de una agonía ardiente,
suicida!

Hay ganas de . . . no tener ganas. Señor;
a ti yo te señalo con el dedo deicida;
hay ganas de no haber tenido corazón.

La primavera vuelve, vuelve y se irá. Y Dios,
curvado en tiempo, se repite, y pasa, pasa
a cuestas con la espina dorsal del Universo.

Cuando las sienes tocan su lúgubre tambor,
cuando me duele el sueño grabado en un puñal,
¡hay ganas de quedarse plantado en este verso!

THE WEARY CIRCLES

There are desires to return, to love, not to go away,
and there are desires to die, fought by two
opposite waters that will never become isthmus.

There are desires for a kiss that would shroud life,
that withers in Africa of a fiery agony,
suicide!

There are desires to . . . not have desires. Lord,
at you I point my god-murdering finger.
There are desires not to have had a heart at all.

Spring returns; it returns and will go away. And God
curved in time repeats himself, and passes, passes
with the backbone of the universe on his shoulder.

When my temples beat their mournful drum,
when that sleep etched on a knife hurts me,
there are desires not to move an inch from this poem!

Translated by John Knoepfle

DIOS

Siento a Dios que camina
tan en mí, con la tarde y con el mar.
Con él nos vamos juntos. Anochece.
Con él anochecemos, Orfandad . . .

Pero yo siento a Dios. Y hasta parece
que él me dicta no sé que buen color.
Como un hospitalario, es bueno y triste;
mustia un dulce desdén de enamorado:
debe dolerle mucho el corazón.

Oh, Dios mío, recién a ti me llego,
hoy que amo tanto en esta tarde; hoy
que en la falsa balanza de unos senos,
mido y lloro una frágil Creación.

Y tú, cuál llorarás . . . tú, enamorado
de tanto enorme seno girador . . .
Yo te consagro Dios, porque amas tanto;
porque jamás sonríes: porque siempre
debe dolerte mucho el corazón.

GOD

I feel that God is traveling
so much in me, with the dusk and the sea.
With him we go along together. It is getting dark.
With him we get dark. All orphans . . .

But I feel God. And it even seems
that he sets aside some good color for me.
He is kind and sad, like those who care for the sick;
he whispers with sweet contempt like a lover's:
his heart must give him great pain.

Oh, my God, I've only just come to you,
today I love so much in this twilight; today
that in the false balance of some breasts
I weigh and weep for a frail Creation.

And you, what do you weep for . . . you, in love
with such an immense and whirling breast. . . .
I consecrate you, God, because you love so much;
because you never smile; because your heart
must all the time give you great pain.

Translated by Robert Bly

LOS ARRIEROS

Arriero, vas fabulosamente vidriado de sudor.
La hacienda Menocucho
cobra mil sinsabores diarios por la vida.
Las doce. Vamos a la cintura del día.
El sol que duele mucho.

Arriero, con tu poncho colorado te alejas,
saboreando el romance peruano de tu coca.
Y yo desde una hamaca,
desde un siglo de duda,
cavilo tu horizonte y atisbo, lamentado,
por zancudos, y por el estribillo gentil
y enfermo de una "paca-paca".
Al fin tú llegarás donde debes llegar,
arriero, que, detrás de tu burro santurrón,
te vas . . .
te vas . . .

Feliz de ti, en este calor en que se encabritan
todas las ansias y todos los motivos;
cuando el espíritu que anima al cuerpo apenas,
va sin coca, y no atina a cabestrar
su bruto hacia los Andes
occidentales de la Eternidad.

THE MULE DRIVERS

Mule driver, you walk along fantastically glazed with
    sweat.
The Menocucho ranch charges
daily one thousand troubles for life.
Twelve noon. We've arrived at the waist of the day.
The sun that hurts so much.

Mule driver, you gradually vanish with your red poncho,
enjoying the Peruvian folksong of your coca leaves.
And I, from a hammock,
from a century of irresolution,
brood over your horizon, mourned for
by mosquitoes, and by the delicate
and feeble song of a paca-paca bird.
In the end you'll arrive where you are supposed to arrive,
mule driver, behind your saintly burro, going
away . . .
away . . .

You are lucky then, in this heat in which
all our desires and all our intentions rear up;
when the spirit that hardly rouses the body
walks without coca, and does not succeed in pulling
its brute toward the western
Andes of Eternity.

Translated by Robert Bly

LOS PASOS LEJANOS

Mi padre duerme. Su semblante augusto
figura un apacible corazón;
está ahora tan dulce . . .
si hay algo en él de amargo, seré yo.

Hay soledad en el hogar; se reza;
y no hay noticias de los hijos hoy.
Mi padre se despierta, ausculta
la huída a Egipto, el restañante adiós.
Está ahora tan cerca;
si hay algo en él de lejos, seré yo.

Y mi madre pasea allá en los huertos,
saboreando un sabor ya sin sabor.
Está ahora tan suave,
tan ala, tan salida, tan amor.

Hay soledad en el hogar sin bulla,
sin noticias, sin verde, sin niñez.
Y si hay algo quebrado en esta tarde,
y que baja y que cruje,
son dos viejos caminos blancos, curvos.
Por ellos va mi corazón a pie.

THE DISTANT FOOTSTEPS

My father is sleeping. His noble face
suggests a mild heart;
he is so sweet now . . .
if anything bitter is in him, I must be the bitterness.

There is loneliness in the parlor; they are praying;
and there is no news of the children today.
My father wakes, he listens
for the flight into Egypt, the good-bye that dresses
    wounds.
Now he is so near;
if anything distant is in him, I must be the distance.

And my mother walks past in the orchard,
savoring a taste already without savor.
Now she is so gentle,
so much wing, so much farewell, so much love.

There is loneliness in the parlor with no sound,
no news, no greenness, no childhood.
And if something is broken this afternoon,
and if something descends or creaks,
it is two old roads, curving and white.
Down them my heart is walking on foot.

Translated by James Wright
and John Knoepfle

A MI HERMANO MIGUEL

in memoriam

Hermano, hoy estoy en el poyo de la casa,
donde nos haces una falta sin fondo!
Me acuerdo que jugábamos esta hora, y que mamá
nos acariciaba: "Pero, hijos . . ."

Ahora yo me escondo,
como antes, todas estas oraciones
vespertinas, y espero que tú no des conmigo.
Por la sala, el zaguán, los corredores.
Después, te ocultas tú, y yo no doy contigo.
Me acuerdo que nos hacíamos llorar,
hermano, en aquel juego.

Miguel, tú te escondiste
una noche de agosto, al alborear;
pero, en ves de ocultarte riendo, estabas triste.
Y tu gemelo corazón de esas tardes
extintas se ha aburrido de no encontrarte. Y ya
cae sombra en el alma.

Oye hermano, no tardes
en salir. Bueno? Puede inquietarse mamá.

TO MY BROTHER MIGUEL

in memoriam

Brother, today I sit on the brick bench outside the house,
where you make a bottomless emptiness.
I remember we used to play at this hour of the day, and
    mama
would calm us: "There now, boys . . ."

Now I go hide
as before, from all these evening
prayers, and I hope that you will not find me.
In the parlor, the entrance hall, the corridors.
Later, you hide, and I do not find you.
I remember we made each other cry,
brother, in that game.

Miguel, you hid yourself
one night in August, nearly at daybreak,
but instead of laughing when you hid, you were sad.
And your other heart of those dead afternoons
is tired of looking and not finding you. And now
shadows fall on the soul.

Listen, brother, don't be too late
coming out. All right? Mama might worry.

Translated by John Knoepfle
and James Wright

ESPERGESIA

Yo nací un día
que Dios estuvo enfermo.

Todos saben que vivo,
que soy malo; y no saben
del diciembre de ese enero.
Pues yo nací un día
que Dios estuvo enfermo.

Hay un vacío
en mi aire metafísco
que nadie ha de palpar:
el claustro de un silencio
que habló a flor de fuego.

Yo nací un día
que Dios estuvo enfermo.

Hermano, escucha, escucha . . .
Bueno. Y que no me vaya
sin llevar diciembres,
sin dejar eneros.
Pues yo nací un día
que Dios estuvo enfermo.

Todos saben que vivo,
que mastico . . . Y no saben
por qué en mi verso chirrian,
oscuro sinsabor de féretro,
luyidos vientos
desenroscados de la Esfinge
preguntona del Desierto.

HAVE YOU ANYTHING TO SAY
IN YOUR DEFENSE?

Well, on the day I was born,
God was sick.

They all know that I'm alive,
that I'm vicious; and they don't know
the December that follows from that January.
Well, on the day I was born,
God was sick.

There is an empty place
in my metaphysical shape
that no one can reach:
a cloister of silence
that spoke with the fire of its voice muffled.

On the day I was born,
God was sick.

Brother, listen to me, Listen . . .
Oh, all right. Don't worry, I won't leave
without taking my Decembers along,
without leaving my Januaries behind.
Well, on the day I was born,
God was sick.

They all know that I'm alive,
that I chew my food . . . and they don't know
why harsh winds whistle in my poems,
the narrow uneasiness of a coffin,
winds untangled from the Sphinx
who holds the desert for routine questioning.

Todos saben . . . Y no saben
que la Luz es tísica,
y la Sombra gorda . . .
Y no saben que el Misterio sintetiza . . .
que él es la joroba
musical y triste que a distancia denuncia
el paso meridiano de las lindes a las Lindes

Yo nací un día
que Dios estuvo enfermo,
grave.

Yes, they all know . . . Well, they don't know
that the light gets skinny
and the darkness gets bloated . . .
and they don't know that the Mystery joins things
     together . . .
that he is the hunchback
musical and sad who stands a little way off and foretells
the dazzling progression from the limits to the Limits.

On the day I was born,
God was sick,
gravely.

Translated by James Wright

from

Trilce

1922

Las personas mayores
¿a qué hora volverán?
Da la seis el ciego Santiago,
y ya está muy oscuro.

Madre dijo que no demoraría.

Aguedita, Nativa, Miguel,
cuidado con ir por ahí, por donde
acaban de pasar gangueando sus memorias
dobladoras penas,
hacia el silencioso corral, y por donde
las gallinas que se están aconstando todavía,
se han espantado tanto.
Mejor estemos aquí no más.
Madre dijo que no demoraría.

Ya no tengamos pena. Vamos viendo
los barcos ¡el mío es más bonito de todos!
con los cuales jugamos todo el santo día,
sin pelearnos, como debe ser:
han quedado en el pozo de agua, listos,
fletados de dulces para mañana.

Aguardemos así, obedientes y sin más
remedio, la vuelta, el desagravio
de los mayores siempre delanteros
dejándonos en casa a los pequeños,
como si también nosotros no pudiésemos partir.

III

What time are the big people
going to come back?
Blind Santiago is striking six
and already it's very dark.

Mother said that she wouldn't be delayed.

Aguedita, Nativa, Miguel
be careful of going over there, where
doubled-up griefs whimpering their memories
have just gone
toward the quiet poultry-yard, where
the hens are still getting settled,
who have been startled so much.
We'd better just stay here.
Mother said that she wouldn't be delayed.

And we shouldn't be sad. Let's go see
the boats—mine is prettier than anybody's!—
we were playing with them the whole blessed day,
without fighting among ourselves, as it should be:
they stayed behind in the puddle, all ready,
loaded with pleasant things for tomorrow.

Let's wait like this, obedient
and helpless, for the homecoming, the apologies
of the big people, who are always the first
to abandon the rest of us in the house—
as if we couldn't get away too!

Aguedita, Nativa, Miguel?
Llamo, busco al tanteo en la oscuridad.
No me vayan a haber dejado solo,
y el único recluso sea yo.

Aguedita, Nativa, Miguel?
I am calling, I am feeling around for you in the darkness.
Don't leave me behind by myself,
to be locked in all alone.

Translated by James Wright

XV

En el rincón aquel, donde dormimos juntos
tantas noches, ahora me he sentado
a caminar. La cuja de los novios difuntos
fue sacada, o talvez qué habrá pasado.

Has venido temprano a otros asuntos
y ya no estás. Es el rincón
donde a tu lado, leí una noche,
entre tus tiernos puntos,
un cuento de Daudet. Es el rincón
amado. No lo equivoques.

Me he puesto a recordar los días
de verano idos, tu entrar y salir,
poca y harta y pálida por los cuartos.

En esta noche pluviosa,
ya lejos de ambos dos, salto de pronto . . .
Son dos puertas abriéndose cerrándose,
dos puertas que al viento van y vienen
sombra   a   sombra.

XV

In that corner, where we slept together
so many nights, I've sat down now
to take a walk. The bedstead of the dead lovers
has been taken away, or what could have happened.

You came early for other things,
but you're gone now. This is the corner
where I read one night, by your side,
between your tender breasts,
a story by Daudet. It is the corner
we loved. Don't confuse it with any other.

I've started to think about those days
of summer gone, with you entering and leaving,
little and fed up, pale through the rooms.

On this rainy night,
already far from both of us, all at once I jump . . .
There are two doors, swinging open, shut,
two doors in the wind, back, and forth,
shadow   to   shadow.

Translated by James Wright

XXIV

Al borde de un sepulcro florecido
trascurren dos marías llorando,
llorando a mares.

El ñandú desplumado del recuerdo
alarga su postrera pluma,
y con ella la mano negativa de Pedro
graba en un domingo de ramos
resonancias de exequias y de piedras.

Del borde de un sepulcro removido
se alejan dos marías cantando.

Lunes.

XXIV

At the border of a flowering grave,
two marys go into the past, weeping,
weeping whole seas.

The ostrich stripped of its memory
stretches out its last feather,
and with it the denying hand of Peter
carves on Palm Sunday
resonances of funeral services and stones.

From the border of a stirred-up grave
two marys drift away, singing.

Monday.

Translated by James Wright

XLV

Me desvinculo del mar
cuando vienen las aguas a mí.

Salgamos siempre. Saboreemos
la canción estupenda, la canción dicha
por los labios inferiores del deseo.
Oh prodigiosa doncellez.
Pasa la brisa sin sal.

A los lejos husmeo los tuétanos
oyendo el tanteo profundo, a la caza
de teclas de resaca.

Y si así diéramos las narices
en el absurdo,
nos cubriremos con el oro de no tener nada,
y empollaremos el ala aún no nacida
de la noche, hermana
de esta ala huérfana del día,
que a fuerza de ser una ya no es ala.

XLV

I am freed from the burdens of the sea
when the waters come toward me.

Let us always sail out. Let us taste
the marvelous song, the song spoken
by the lower lips of desire.
Oh beautiful virginity.
The saltless breeze passes.

From the distance, I breathe marrows,
hearing the profound score, as the surf
hunts for its keys.

And if we banged
into the absurd,
we shall cover ourselves with the gold of owning nothing,
and hatch the still unborn wing
of the night, sister
of the orphaned wing of the day,
that is not really a wing since it is only one.

Translated by James Wright

LXXVII

Graniza tanto, como para que yo recuerde
y acreciente las perlas
que he recogido del hocico mismo
de cada tempestad.

No se vaya a secar esta lluvia.
A menos que me fuese dado
caer ahora para ella, o que me enterrasen
mojado en el agua
que surtiera de todos los fuegos.

¿Hasta dónde me alcanzará esta lluvia?
Temo me quede con algún flanco seco;
temo que ella se vaya, sin haberme probado
en las sequías de increíbles cuerdas vocales,
por las que
para dar armonía,
hay siempre que subir ¡nunca bajar!
¿No subimos acaso para abajo?

Canta, lluvia, en la costa aún sin mar!

LXXVII

So much hail that I remember,
and pile on a few pearls
to those I have pulled right from under
the snout of the other storms.

I don't want this rain to dry up.
At least not unless they let me fall
right now instead of it, or unless they buried me
soaked in the water
shooting up from every fire in the world.

I wonder where the water-line on my body will be?
I'm afraid I'll be left with one of my sides dry.
I'm afraid the rain will end before I'm tested
in the bone-dry months of the incredible vocal chords,
where to create harmony
we have to rise always! and never go down!
Well, don't we rise, really, to go down?

Sing on, rain, on this coast still with no sea!

Translated by Robert Bly
and James Wright

from

Codigo Civil
and
Poemas Humanos

1939

EL BUEN SENTIDO

—Hay, madre, un sitio en el mundo, que se llama París. Un sitio muy grande y lejano y otra vez grande.

Mi madre me ajusta el cuello del abrigo, no por que empieza a nevar, sino para que empiece a nevar.

La mujer de mi padre está enamorada de mí, viniendo y avanzando de espaldas a mi nacimiento y de pecho a mi muerte. Que soy dos veces suyo: por el adiós y por el regreso. La cierro, al retornar. Por eso me dieran tánto sus ojos, justa de mí, infraganti de mí, aconteciéndose por obras terminadas, por pactos consumados.

¿Mi madre está confesa de mí, nombrada de mí? ¿Cómo no da otro tanto a mis otros hermanos? A Víctor, por ejemplo, el mayor, que es tan viejo ya, que las gentes dicen: ¡Parece hermano menor de su padre! ¡Fuere porque yo he viajado mucho! ¡Fuere porque yo he vivido más!

Mi madre acuerda carta de principio colorante a mis relatos de regreso. Ante mi vida de regreso, recordando que viajé durante dos corazones por su vientre, se ruboriza y se queda mortalmente lívida, cuando digo, en el tratado del alma: Aquella noche fuí dichoso. Pero más se pone triste; más se pusiera triste.

—Hijo, ¡cómo estás viejo!

"Mother, you know there is a place somewhere called
Paris. It's a huge place and a long way off and it really
is huge."

My mother turns up my coat collar, not because it's
starting to snow, but in order that it may start.

My father's wife is in love with me, walking up, always
keeping her back to my birth, and her face toward my
death. Because I am hers twice: by my good-bye and
by my coming home. When I return home, I close her.
That is why her eyes gave me so much, pronounced inno-
cent of me, caught in the act of me, everything occurs
through finished arrangements, through covenants car-
ried out.

Has my mother confessed me, has she been named pub-
licly? Why doesn't she give so much to my other broth-
ers? To Victor, for example, the oldest, who is so old now
that people say, "He looks like his father's youngest
brother!" It must be because I have traveled so much! It
must be because I have lived more!

My mother gives me illuminated permissions to explore
my coming-home tales. Face to face with my returning-
home life, remembering that I journeyed for two whole
hearts through her womb, she blushes and goes deathly
pale when I say in the discourse of the soul: "That night
I was happy!" But she grows more sad, she grew more
sad.

"How old you're getting, son!"

Y desfila por el color amarillo a llorar, porque me halla envejecido, en la hoja de espada, en la desembocadura de mi rostro. Llora de mí, se entristece de mí. ¿Qué falta hará mi mocedad, si siempre seré su hijo? ¿Por qué las madres se duelen de hallar envejecidos a sus hijos, si jamás la edad de ellos alcanzará a la de ellas? ¿Y por qué, si los hijos, cuanto más se acaban, más se aproximan a los padres? ¡Mi madre llora porque estoy viejo de mi tiempo y porque nunca llegaré a envejecer del suyo!

Mi adiós partió de un punto de su ser, más externo que el punto de su ser al que retorno. Soy, a causa del excesivo plazo de mi vuelta, más el hombre ante mi madre que el hijo ante mi madre. Allí reside el candor que hoy nos alumbra con tres llamas. Le digo entonces hasta que me callo:

—Hay, madre, en el mundo, un sitio que se llama París. Un sitio muy grande y muy lejano y otra vez grande.

La mujer de mi padre, al oírme, almuerza y sus ojos mortales descienden suavemente por mis brazos.

And she walks firmly through the color yellow to cry, because I seem to her to be getting old, on the blade of the sword, in the delta of my face. Weeps with me, grows sad with me. Why should my youth be necessary, if I will always be her son? Why do mothers feel pain when their sons get old, if their age will never equal anyway the age of the mothers? And why, if the sons, the more they get on, merely come nearer to the age of the fathers? My mother cries because I am old in my time and because I will never get old enough to be old in hers!

My good-byes left from a point in her being more toward the outside than the point in her being to which I come back. I am, because I am so overdue coming back, more the man to my mother than the son to my mother. The purity that lights us both now with three flames lies precisely in that. I say then until I finally fall silent:

"Mother, you know there is a place somewhere called Paris. It's a huge place and a long way off and it really is huge."

The wife of my father, hearing my voice, goes on eating her lunch, and her eyes that will die descend gently along my arms.

Translated by Robert Bly

VOY A HABLAR DE LA ESPERANZA

Yo no sufro este dolor como César Vallejo. Yo no me duelo ahora como artista, como hombre ni como simple ser vivo siquiera. Yo no sufro este dolor como católico, como mahometano ni como ateo. Hoy sufro solamente. Si no me llamase César Vallejo, también sufriría este mismo dolor. Si no fuese artista, también lo sufriría. Si no fuese católico, ateo ni mahometano, también lo sufriría. Hoy sufro desde más abajo. Hoy sufro solamente.

Me duelo ahora sin explicaciones. Mi dolor es tan hondo, que no tuvo ya causa ni carece de causa. ¿Qué sería su causa? ¿Dónde está aquello tan importante, que dejase de ser su causa? Nada es su causa; nada ha podido dejar de ser su causa. ¿A qué ha nacido este dolor, por sí mismo? Mi dolor es del viento del norte y del viento del sur, como esos huevos neutros que algunas aves raras ponen del viento. Si hubiera muerto mi novia, mi dolor sería igual. Si me hubieran cortado el cuello de raíz, mi dolor sería igual. Si la vida fuese, en fin, de otro modo, mi dolor sería igual. Hoy sufro desde más arriba. Hoy sufro solamente.

Miro el dolor del hambriento y veo que su hambre anda tan lejos de mi sufrimiento, que de quedarme ayuno hasta morir, saldría siempre de mi tumba una brizna de yerba al menos. ¡Lo mismo el enamorado! ¡Qué sangre la suya más engendrada, para la mía sin fuente ni consumo!

I AM GOING TO TALK ABOUT HOPE

I do not feel this suffering as César Vallejo. I am not suffering now as a creative person, or as a man, nor even as a simple living being. I don't feel this pain as a Catholic, or as a Mohammedan, or as an atheist. Today I am simply in pain. If my name weren't César Vallejo, I'd still feel it. If I weren't an artist, I'd still feel it. If I weren't a man, or even a living being, I'd still feel it. If I weren't a Catholic, or an atheist, or a Mohammedan, I'd still feel it. Today I am in pain from further down. Today I am simply in pain.

The pain I have has no explanations. My pain is so deep that it never had a cause, and has no need of a cause. What could its cause have been? Where is that thing so important that it stopped being its cause? Its cause is nothing, and nothing could have stopped being its cause. Why has this pain been born all on its own? My pain comes from the north wind and from the south wind, like those hermaphrodite eggs that some rare birds lay conceived of the wind. If my bride were dead, my suffering would still be the same. If they had slashed my throat all the way through, my suffering would still be the same. If life, in other words, were different, my suffering would still be the same. Today I'm in pain from higher up. Today I am simply in pain.

I look at the hungry man's pain, and I see that his hunger walks somewhere so far from my pain that if I fasted until death, one blade of grass at least would always sprout from my grave. And the same with the lover! His blood is too fertile for mine, which has no source and no one to drink it.

Yo creía hasta ahora que todas las cosas del universo eran, inevitablemente, padres o hijos. Pero he aquí que mi dolor de hoy no es padre ni es hijo. Le falta espalda para anochecer, tanto como le sobra pecho para amanecer y si lo pusiesen en la estancia oscura, no daría luz y si lo pusiesen en una estancia luminosa, no echaría sombra. Hoy sufro suceda lo que suceda. Hoy sufro solamente.

I always believed up till now that all things in the world had to be either fathers or sons. But here is my pain that is neither a father nor a son. It hasn't any back to get dark, and it has too bold a front for dawning, and if they put it into some dark room, it wouldn't give light, and if they put it into some brightly lit room, it wouldn't cast a shadow. Today I am in pain, no matter what happens. Today I am simply in pain.

Translated by Robert Bly

Quédeme a calentar la tinta en que me ahogo
y a escuchar mi caverna alternativa,
noches de tacto, días de abstracción.

Se estremeció la incógnita en mi amígdala
y crují de una anual melancolía,
noches de sol, días de luna, ocasos de París.

Y todavía, hoy mismo, al atardecer,
digiero sacratísimas constancias,
noches de madre, días de biznieta
bicolor, voluptuosa, urgente, linda.

Y aún
alcanzo, llego hasta mí en avión de dos asientos,
bajo la mañana doméstica y la bruma
que emergió eternamente de un instante.

Y todavía,
aún ahora,
al cabo del cometa en que he ganado
mi bacilo feliz y doctoral,
he aquí que caliente, oyente, tierro, sol y luno,
incógnito atravieso el cementerio,
tomo a la izquierda, hiendo
la yerba con un par de endecasílabos,
años de tumba, litros de infinito,
tinta, pluma, ladrillos y perdones.

24 septiembre 1937

I stayed here, warming the ink in which I drown,
and listening to my other cavern,
nights of touch, days of mental drifting.

Something unknown quivered in my tonsils,
and I creaked with my annual melancholy,
nights of sunlight, days of moonlight, sunsets of Paris.

And yet, even today, at the fall of evening,
I digest the most holy loyalties,
nights of the mother, days of the great-granddaughter,
two-colored, voluptuous, urgent, charming.

Nevertheless
I do come abreast, I overtake myself in a two-seater air-
    plane,
under the domestic morning, and the fog
that crept out of a second forever and ever.

And yet,
even now,
inside the tail of the comet in which I've won
my happy PhD germ,
here I am, burning, listening, masculine-earthlike, sun-
    like, masculine-moonlike,
I cross the graveyard unrecognized,
swerve to the left, cutting
the grass with a pair of hendecasyllabics,
years in the sepulcher, liters of infinity,
ink, pen, bricks, and forgivings.

Translated by James Wright
and Robert Bly

POEMA PARA SER LEIDO Y CANTADO

Sé que hay una persona
que me busca en su mano, día y noche,
encontrándome, a cada minuto, en su calzado.
Ignora que la noche está enterrada
con espuelas detrás de la cocina?

Sé que hay una persona compuesta de mis partes,
a la que integro cuando va mi talle
cabalgando en su exacta piedrecilla.
Ignora que a su cofre
no volverá moneda que salió con su retrato?

Sé el día,
pero el sol se me ha escapado;
sé el acto universal que hizo en su cama
con ajeno valor y esa agua tibia, cuya
superficial frecuencia es una mina.
Tan pequeña es, acaso, esa persona,
que hasta sus propios pies así la pisan?

Un gato es el lindero entre ella y yo,
al lado mismo de su taza de agua.
La veo en las esquinas, se abre y cierra
su veste, antes palmera interrogante . .
Qué podrá hacer sino cambiar de llanto?

Pero me busca y busca. Es una historia!

POEM TO BE READ AND SUNG

    I know there is someone
looking for me day and night inside her hand,
and coming upon me, each moment, in her shoes.
Doesn't she know the night is buried
with spurs behind the kitchen?

    I know there is someone composed of my pieces,
whom I complete when my waist
goes galloping on her precise little stone.
Doesn't she know that money once out for her likeness
never returns to her trunk?

    I know the day,
but the sun has escaped from me;
I know the universal act she performed in her bed
with some other woman's bravery and warm water, whose
shallow recurrence is a mine.
Is it possible this being is so small
even her own feet walk on her that way?

    A cat is the border between us two,
right there beside her bowl of water.
I see her on the corners, her dress—once
an inquiring palm tree—opens and closes. . . .
What can she do but change her style of weeping?

But she does look and look for me. This is a real story!

*Translated by James Wright
and Robert Bly*

PIEDRA NEGRA SOBRE UNA
PIEDRA BLANCA

Me moriré en Paris con aguacero,
un día del cual tengo ya el recuerdo.
Me moriré en Paris—y no me corro—
tal vez un jueves, como es hoy, de otoño.

Jueves será, porque hoy, jueves, que proso
estos versos, los húmeros me he puesto
a la mala y, jamás como hoy, me he vuelto,
con todo mi camino, a verme solo.

César Vallejo ha muerto, le pegaban
todos sin que él les haga nada;
le daban duro con un palo y duro

también con una soga; son testigos
los días jueves y los huesos húmeros,
la soledad, la lluvia, los caminos . . .

BLACK STONE LYING ON A
WHITE STONE

I will die in Paris, on a rainy day,
on some day I can already remember.
I will die in Paris—and I don't step aside—
perhaps on a Thursday, as today is Thursday, in au-
    tumn.

It will be a Thursday, because today, Thursday, set-
    ting down
these lines, I have put my upper arm bones on
wrong, and never so much as today have I found myself
with all the road ahead of me, alone.

César Vallejo is dead. Everyone beat him,
although he never does anything to them;
they beat him hard with a stick and hard also

with a rope. These are the witnesses:
the Thursdays, and the bones of my arms,
the solitude, and the rain, and the roads . . .

Translated by Robert Bly
and John Knoepfle

NOMINA DE HUESOS

Se pedía a grandes voces:
—Que muestre las dos manos a la vez.
Y esto no fué posible.
—Que, mientras llora, le tomen la medida de sus pasos
Y esto no fué posible.
—Que piense un pensamiento idéntico, en el tiempo que
    un cero permanece inútil.
Y esto no fué posible.
—Que haga una locura.
Y esto no fué posible.
—Que entre él y otro hombre semejante a él, ponga una
    muchedumbre de hombres como él.
Y esto no fué posible.
—Que le comparen consigo mismo.
Y esto no fué posible.
—Que le llamen, en fin, por su nombre.
Y esto no fué posible.

THE ROLLCALL OF BONES

They demanded in loud voices:
"We want him to show both hands at the same time."
And that simply couldn't be done.
"We want them to check the length of his steps while he
    cries."
And that simply couldn't be done.
"We want him to think one identical thought during the
    time a zero goes on being useless."
And that simply couldn't be done.
"We want him to do something crazy."
And that simply couldn't be done.
"We want a mass of men like him to stand in between him
    and another man just like him."
And that simply couldn't be done.
"We want them to compare him with himself."
And that simply couldn't be done.
"We want them to call him finally by his own name."
And that simply couldn't be done.

Translated by Robert Bly

En el momento en que el tenista lanza magistralmente
su bala, le posee una inocencia totalmente animal;
en el momento
en que el filósofo sorprende una nueva verdad,
es una bestia completa.
Anatole France afirmaba
que el sentimiento religioso
es la función de un órgano especial del cuerpo humano,
hasta ahora ignorado y se podría
decir también, entonces,
que, en el momento exacto en que un tal órgano
funciona plenamente
tan puro de malicia está el creyente,
que se diría casi un vegetal.
¡Oh alma! ¡Oh pensamiento! ¡Oh Marx! ¡Oh Feuerbach!

The tennis-player, in the instant he majestically
serves his ball, he has an innocence almost totally animal;
in the instant the philosopher
surprises a new truth
he's an absolute brute.
Anatole France tells us
the religious emotion
is secreted by a special organ of the human body,
up till now unrecognized,
in fact it's possible to declare further
that at precisely the moment in which that organ
is functioning perfectly
the believer is so marvelously wicked
as to be almost a vegetable.
Oh soul! Oh thinking! Oh Marx! Oh Feuerbach!

Translated by Robert Bly

Un pilar soportando consuelos,
pilar otro,
pilar en duplicado, pilaroso
y como nieto de una puerta oscura.
Ruido perdido, el uno, oyendo, al borde del cansancio;
bebiendo, el otro, dos a dos, con asas.

¿Ignoro acaso el año de este día,
el odio de este amor, las tablas de esta frente?
¿Ignoro que esta tarde cuesta días?
¿Ignoro que jamás se dice "nunca," de rodillas?

Los pilares que ví me están oyendo;
otros pilares son, doses y nietos tristes de mi pierna.
¡Lo digo en cobre americano,
que le bebe a la plata tanto fuego!

Consolado en terceras nupcias,
pálido, nacido,
voy a cerrar mi pila bautismal, esta vidriera,
este susto con tetas,
este dedo en capilla,
corazonmente unido a mi esqueleto.

6 septiembre 1937

One pillar holding up consolations,
another pillar,
a pillar in duplicate, a pillar
like the grandson of a dark door.
Lost outcries, the one listening at the edge of exhaustion;
the other pillar, with handles, drinking, two by two.

Perhaps I don't know this day of the year,
the hatred of this love, the slabs of this forehead?
Don't I know that this afternoon will cost days?
Don't I know that one never says "never" on his knees?

The pillars that I looked at are listening to me;
they are other pillars, pairs of them, sad grandsons of
     my leg.
I say it in American copper:
that drinks so much fire from the silver!

Consoled by third marriages,
pale, just born,
I am going to lock my baptismal font, this glass showcase,
this fear that has breasts,
this fingertip with the hood on,
in my heart united with my skeleton.

Translated by James Wright

Y no me digan nada,
que uno puede matar perfectamente,
ya que, sudando tinta,
uno hace cuanto puede, no me digan . . .

Volveremos, señores, a vernos con manzanas;
tarde la criatura pasará,
la expresión de Aristóteles armada
de grandes corazones de madera,
la de Heráclito injerta en la de Marx,
la del suave sonando rudamente . . .
Es lo que bien narraba mi garganta:
uno puede matar perfectamente.

Señores,
caballeros, volveremos a vernos sin paquetes;
hasta entonces exijo, exigiré de mi flaqueza
el acento del día, que
según veo, estuvo ya esperándome en mi lecho.
Y exijo del sombrero la infausta analogía del recuerdo,
ya que, a veces, asumo con éxito mi inmensidad llorada,
ya que, a veces, me ahogo en la voz de mi vecino
y padezco
contando en maíces los años,
cepillando mi ropa al son de un muerto
o sentado borracho en mi ataúd . . .

Hacia 1937

And don't bother telling me anything,
that a man can kill perfectly,
because a man,
sweating ink, does what he can, don't bother telling
    me . . .

Gentlemen, we'll see ourselves with apples again,
the infant will go by at last,
the expression of Aristotle fortified
with huge wooden hearts,
and Heraclitus's grafted on to Marx's,
the suave one's sounding abrupt . . .
My own throat used to tell me that all the time:
a man can kill perfectly.

Sirs
and gentlemen, we'll see ourselves without packages
    again;
until that time I ask, from my inadequacy I would like
    to know
the day's tone, which,
as I see it, has already been here waiting for me in my
    bed.
And I demand of my hat the doomed analogy of memory,
since at times I assume my wept-for and immense space,
    successfully,
since at times I drown in the voice of my neighbor,
and I suffer
counting the years like corn grains,
brushing off my clothes to the sound of a corpse,
or sitting drunk in my coffin. . . .

Translated by Robert Bly

257

¿Y bien? ¿Te sana el metaloide pálido?
¿Los metaloides incendiarios, cívicos,
inclinados al río atroz del polvo?

Esclavo, es ya la hora circular
en que las dos aurículas se forman
anillos guturales, corredizos, cuaternarios.

Señor esclavo, en la mañana mágica
se ve, por fin,
el busto de tu trémulo ronquido,
vense tus sufrimientos a caballo,
pasa el órgano bueno, el de tres asas,
hojeo, mes por mes, tu monocorde cabellera,
tu suegra llora
haciendo huesecillos de sus dedos,
se inclina tu alma con pasión a verte
y tu sien, un momento, marca el paso.

Y la gallina pone su infinito, uno por uno;
sale la tierra hermosa de las humeantes sílabas,
te retratas de pie junto a tu hermano,
truena el color oscuro bajo el lecho
y corren y entrechócanse los pulpos.

Señor esclavo, ¿y bien?
¿Los metaloides obran en tu angustia?

27 septiembre 1937

And so? The pale metalloid heals you?
The flammable metalloids, civilized,
leaning toward the hideous river of dust?

Slave, it's now the huge round hour
when the two auricles make
guttural rings, slippery, post-Tertiary.

Esquire slave, the bust of your quivery snore
is visible at last
in the enchanted morning,
your suffering is seen on horseback,
the good organ goes by—-the one with three ears—,
I leaf month after month through your long one-stringed
        hair,
your mother-in-law sobs
as she makes tiny bones from her fingers,
your soul bends madly over to see you
and for an instant your temple keeps time.

And the hen lays her infinite, one by one;
handsome earth rises from the smoking syllables,
you get photographed standing by your brother,
the shadowy color thunders under the bed,
the octopuses race around and collide.

And so, esquire slave?
Do the metalloids work with your anguish?

Translated by Robert Bly

259

Tengo un miedo terrible de ser un animal
de blanca nieve, que sostuvo padre
y madre, con su sola circulación venosa,
y que, este día espléndido, solar y arzobispal,
día que representa así a la noche,
linealmente
elude este animal estar contento, respirar
y transformarse y tener plata.

Sería pena grande
que fuera yo tan hombre hasta ese punto.
Un disparate, una premisa ubérrima
a cuyo yugo ocasional sucumbe
el gonce espiritual de mi cintura.
Un disparate . . . En tanto,
es así, más acá de la cabeza de Dios,
en la tabla de Locke, de Bacon, en el lívido pescuezo
de la bestia, en el hocico del alma.

Y, en lógica aromática,
tengo ese miedo práctico, este día
espléndido, lunar, de ser aquél, éste talvez,
a cuyo olfato huele a muerto el suelo,
el disparate vivo y el disparate muerto.

¡Oh revolcarse, estar, toser, fajarse,
fajarse la doctrina, la sien, de un hombro al otro,
alejarse, llorar, darlo por ocho
o por siete o por seis, por cinco o darlo
por la vida que tiene tres potencias!

22 octubre 1937

I have a terrible fear of being an animal
of white snow, who has kept his father and mother
alive with his solitary circulation through the veins,
and a fear that on this day which is so marvelous, sunny,
        archbishoprical,
(a day that stands so for night)
this animal, like a straight line,
will manage not to be happy, or to breathe,
or to turn into something else, or to get money.

    It would be a terrible thing
if I were a lot of man up to that point.
Unthinkable nonsense . . . an overfertile assumption
to whose accidental yoke the spiritual
hinge in my waist succumbs.
Unthinkable. . . . Meanwhile
that's how it is on this side of God's head,
in the tabula of Locke, and of Bacon, in the pale neck
of the beast, in the snout of the soul.

    And, in fragrant logic,
I do have that practical fear, this marvelous
moony day, of being that one, this one maybe,
to whose nose the ground smells like a corpse,
the unthinkable alive and the unthinkable dead.

    Oh to roll on the ground, to be there, to cough, to wrap
        oneself,
to wrap the doctrine, the temple, from shoulder to
        shoulder,
to go away, to cry, to let it go for eight
or for seven or for six, for five, or let it go
for life with its three possibilities!

                              Translated by Robert Bly

¡Y si después de tantas palabras,
no sobrevive la palabra!
¡Si después de las alas de los pájaros,
no sobrevive el pájaro parado!
¡Más valdría, en verdad,
que se lo coman todo y acabemos!

¡Haber nacido para vivir de nuestra muerte!
¡Levantarse del cielo hacia la tierra
por sus propios desastres
y espiar el momento de apagar con su sombra su tiniebla!
¡Más valdría, francamente,
que se lo coman todo y qué más da! . . .

¡Y si después de tanta historia, sucumbimos,
no ya de eternidad,
sino de esas cosas sencillas, como estar
en la casa o ponerse a cavilar!
¡Y si luego encontramos,
de buenas a primeras, que vivimos,
a juzgar por la altura de los astros,
por el peine y las manchas del pañuelo!
¡Más valdría, en verdad,
que se lo coman todo, desde luego!

Se dirá que tenemos
en uno de los ojos mucha pena
y también en el otro, mucha pena
y en los dos, cuando miran, mucha pena . . .
¡Entonces! . . . ¡Claro! . . . Entonces . . . ¡ni palabra!

And what if after so many words,
the word itself doesn't survive!
And what if after so many wings of birds
the stopped bird doesn't survive!
It would be better then, really,
if it were all swallowed up, and let's end it!

To have been born only to live off our own death!
To raise ourselves from the heavens toward the earth
carried up by our own bad luck,
always watching for the moment to put out our darkness
     with our shadow!
It would be better, frankly,
if it were all swallowed up, and the hell with it!

And what if after so much history, we succumb,
not to eternity,
but to these simple things, like being
at home, or starting to brood!
What if we discover later
all of a sudden, that we are living
to judge by the height of the stars
off a comb and off stains on a handkerchief!
It would be better, really,
if it were all swallowed up, right now!

They'll say that we have a lot
of grief in one eye, and a lot of grief
in the other also, and when they look
a lot of grief in both. . . .
So then! . . . Naturally! . . . So! . . . Don't say a
     word!

Translated by Robert Bly
with Douglas Lawder

"LA CÓLERA QUE QUIEBRA AL HOMBRE EN NIÑOS"

La cólera que quiebra al hombre en niños,
que quiebra al niño, en pájaros iguales,
y al pájaro, después, en huevecillos;
la cólera del pobre
tiene un aceite contra dos vinagres.

La cólera que al árbol quiebra en hojas,
a la hoja en botones desiguales
y al botón, en ranuras telescópicas;
la cólera del pobre
tiene dos ríos contra muchos mares.

La cólera que quiebra al bien en dudas,
a la duda, en tres arcos semejantes
y al arco, luego, en tumbas imprevistas;
la cólera del pobre
tiene un acero contra dos puñales.

La cólera que quiebra el alma en cuerpos,
al cuerpo en órganos desemejantes
y al órgano, en octavos pensamientos;
la cólera del pobre
tiene un fuego central contra dos cráteres.

26 octubre 1937

"THE ANGER THAT BREAKS A MAN DOWN INTO BOYS"

The anger that breaks a man down into boys,
that breaks the boy down into equal birds,
and the bird, then, into tiny eggs;
the anger of the poor
owns one smooth oil against two vinegars.

The anger that breaks the tree down into leaves,
and the leaf down into different-sized buds,
and the buds into infinitely fine grooves;
the anger of the poor
owns two rivers against a number of seas.

The anger that breaks the good down into doubts,
and doubt down into three matching arcs,
and the arc, then, into unimaginable tombs;
the anger of the poor
owns one piece of steel against two daggers.

The anger that breaks the soul down into bodies,
the body down into different organs,
and the organ into reverberating octaves of thought;
the anger of the poor
owns one deep fire against two craters.

Translated by Robert Bly

from

Espãna,
Aparta de
Mí Este Cáliz

1940

MASA

Al fin de la batalla,
y muerto el combatiente, vino hacia él un hombre
y le dijo "¡No mueras; te amo tanto!"
Pero el cadáver ¡ay! siguió muriendo.

Se le acercaron dos y repitiéronle:
"¡No nos dejes! ¡Valor! ¡Vuelve a la vida!"
Pero el cadáver ¡ay! siguió muriendo.

Acudieron a él veinte, cien, mil, quinientos mil,
clamando: "¡Tanto amor, y no poder nada contra
     la muerte!"
Pero el cadáver ¡ay! siguió muriendo.

Le rodearon millones de individuos,
con un ruego común: "¡Quédate hermano!"
Pero el cadáver ¡ay! siguió muriendo.

Entonces todos los hombres de la tierra
le rodearon; les vió el cadáver triste, emocionado;
incorporóse lentamente,
abrazó al primer hombre; echóse a andar . . .

10 noviembre 1937

MASSES

When the battle was over,
and the fighter was dead, a man came toward him
and said to him: "Do not die; I love you so!"
But the corpse, it was sad! went on dying.

And two came near, and told him again and again:
"Do not leave us! Courage! Return to life!"
But the corpse, it was sad! went on dying.

Twenty arrived, a hundred, a thousand, five hundred
    thousand,
shouting: "So much love, and it can do nothing against
    death!"
But the corpse, it was sad! went on dying.

Millions of persons stood around him,
all speaking the same thing: "Stay here, brother!"
But the corpse, it was sad! went on dying.

Then all the men on the earth
stood around him; the corpse looked at them sadly,
    deeply moved;
he sat up slowly,
put his arms around the first man; started to walk . . .

November 10, 1937

Translated by Robert Bly